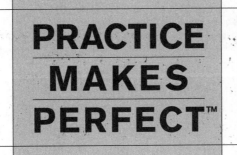

PRACTICE

MAKES

PERFECT™

English Vocabulary for Beginning ESL Learners

Second Edition

Jean Yates

McGraw Hill

New York   Chicago   San Francisco   Lisbon   London   Madrid   Mexico City
Milan   New Delhi   San Juan   Seoul   Singapore   Sydney   Toronto

ISBN   978-0-07-176303-5
MHID   0-07-176303-1

e-ISBN   978-0-07-176304-2
e-MHID   0-07-176304-X

Library of Congress Control Number 2011922817

Contents

Introduction

It is not easy to know how to start learning new words in a language that is not your native one. Most second-language learners depend on a favorite dictionary to get a quick translation of an unknown word; however, dictionaries are full of words that you may never need to use, or even to understand. How do you know which words to learn first?

One of the purposes of this book is to acquaint you with the English words that are most frequently used in the United States today—the words that people use every day with their family, friends, coworkers, and other people in the community in general. Presented here is a basic vocabulary of more than fifteen hundred words that have been carefully chosen because of their frequent appearance and usefulness in daily life. Once you have learned these words and mastered the structures in which they are used, you will be well equipped to add new words to this list, and you'll gradually continue to increase your working vocabulary.

The words of a language can be divided into two groups: content words and function words. Content words in English are either nouns—words that name people, places, things, or abstracts; adjectives—words that describe nouns; verbs—words that describe the actions of nouns; or adverbs—words that describe how an action is performed. Function words are those that form a structure that enables us to put the content words together to make sense. English function words include, for example, words such as *a, the, of, for,* and *and*—words that would be difficult to draw a picture of or to define in a word or two. Both types of words are extremely important for communication in any language.

The second purpose of this book is to provide practice in using content words within the framework of the function words that go with them. By practicing these two types of words together you will be not only learning new vocabulary but also using it correctly, enabling you to form meaningful sentences with a variety of individual words.

There are four sections in the book: Part I: Nouns, Part II: Adjectives, Part III: Verbs, and Part IV: Adverbs. Each of these parts contains a number of units, and each unit consists of special vocabulary for a certain topic and extensive exercises to practice it.

How to Use This Book

The best way to learn new vocabulary is to use it, both in speech and in writing. The exercises in this book are designed to give you that practice by encouraging you to write down exactly what you would say in the context provided. The repetition of words and structures in various types of exercises will help you remember the words and make them yours to use in real situations.

Following are suggestions to help you get the most out of this book:

1. Get a good dictionary, either bilingual or English only, to use as suggested below.
2. Copy on a separate sheet of paper the lists of words presented in each unit.
3. You will already know some of the words. Write a check by each one if you are certain of its meaning.
4. Look up in your dictionary the words that you do not know or are not sure of, and write a word in your language or a definition in English next to it on your paper.
5. Do the written exercises for the entire unit.
6. In the exercises that ask you to write personal sentences, try to use words that are new to you. Of course, if the new words do not fit, use words that you already know.
7. Compare your answers with those in the Answer Key at the back of the book. For the exercises that require personal answers, you may wish to ask a native speaker friend to read your answers to see if they are correct.
8. Go back to your original list, cover up the translations or definitions that you first wrote, and see if you now know all the new words.
9. Try writing more sentences, using the same patterns used in the exercises, to further practice the words that you haven't completely mastered so far.
10. Keep practicing!

PART I

NOUNS

Nouns are the words we use to name all the things we know about, have, see, hear, taste, smell, or feel. This includes words for people, such as *man, teacher,* and *friend.* It includes words for places, such as *city, kitchen,* and *street.* It includes words for things, such as *ball, tree,* and *computer.* And it includes words for things we know exist but can't touch, such as *idea, air, pollution,* and *strength.*

Many nouns can be counted—one friend, two friends, for example. These nouns have plural forms, which in English usually means they have an *-s* added to the end, according to certain set spelling and pronunciation patterns. A few nouns have "irregular" plurals—instead of ending in *-s,* they have forms that have survived from earlier forms of English or were adapted from other languages. Examples of these include *women, men, children, media,* and *phenomena.*

Other nouns cannot be counted—*air, wind,* and *pollution,* for example. They have no plural forms, are used with singular verbs, and are called "noncount" nouns. But noncount nouns can also be things that we can count! First, there are those that it would take a lifetime to count, so we call them by a more general noncount noun, such as *hair, sugar,* or *flour.* And then there are those that we categorize in general groups that are named by noncount nouns, such as *furniture, mail, silverware,* and *china.* Of course we can count *chairs, tables,* or *beds,* but the general category *furniture* is never made plural. The noncount noun *mail* includes the *letters* and *cards* that we can count. English has a lot of these words.

One thing that singular, plural, and noncount nouns have in common is that they can all, in certain situations, be preceded by the article *the. The* before a noun indicates that both the speaker and the hearer know exactly *which one* of the nouns is being referred to. "*The* groceries are in *the* car," for example, informs the hearer that "the groceries that we just bought" are in "the car that we have."

When you know the patterns for using nouns, you can add new ones to your vocabulary every day and know you are using them correctly. Have fun with nouns!

People and Places

Words for People

Members of the Family

Review the words in the following list:

aunt	husband
brother	mother
cousin	nephew
daughter	niece
father	sister
granddaughter	son
grandfather	uncle
grandmother	wife
grandson	

To identify a member of the family of someone's husband or wife, add *in-law* after the relationship word. For example, a man's *mother-in-law* is his wife's mother.

brother-in-law	mother-in-law
daughter-in-law	sister-in-law
father-in-law	son-in-law

exercise 1-1

Fill in each blank with a word from one of the preceding lists.

1. My father's mother is my _____.

2. Her husband is my _____.

3. My mother's sister is my _____.

4. Her husband is my _____.

5. Their daughter is my _____ .

6. My daughter's husband is my _____ .

7. I am a _____ , _____ ,

    _____ , _____ ,

    _____ , and _____ .

8. I have a _____ , _____ ,

    _____ , _____ ,

    _____ , and _____ .

Categories for People

Review the words in the following list:

acquaintance	girl	neighbor
baby	guest	teenager
boy	host	visitor
child	hostess	woman
friend	man	

exercise   1-2

Match each word from the list on the left with its description on the right.

_____ 1. baby   a. a person who lives or works near where you live or work

_____ 2. boy   b. a grown-up female

_____ 3. child   c. a person between the ages of thirteen and nineteen

_____ 4. friend   d. someone you know well and like

_____ 5. girl   e. a grown-up male

_____ 6. man   f. a person under the age of two

_____ 7. neighbor   g. a young male

_____ 8. teenager   h. a young female

_____ 9. woman   i. a person under the age of thirteen

Names of Workers

Review the words in the following list:

accountant	employer	pianist
actor	engineer	pilot
actress	firefighter	police officer
adviser	football player	professor
architect	guide	programmer
artist	hostess	pupil
beautician	janitor	reporter
boss	journalist	sales agent
carpenter	lawyer	sales assistant
cleaner	mail carrier	singer
cook	manager	stewardess
customer	mechanic	student
dancer	military officer	teacher
dentist	nurse	technician
designer	painter	waiter, waitress
director	patient	writer
doctor	pharmacist	
driver	photographer	

exercise 1-3

Circle the word that best completes each sentence.

1. When I am sick I see a ——————————.

   lawyer   carpenter   doctor   police officer

2. The person who gives traffic tickets is a ——————————.

   singer   lawyer   firefighter   police officer

3. The person who lives near my house is my ——————————.

   firefighter   neighbor   military officer   journalist

4. Medicines are prepared at the drugstore by a ——————————.

   mechanic   nurse   pharmacist   sales assistant

5. If I have a toothache, I see a ——————————.

   janitor   doctor   dentist   technician

Parts of the Body

Review the words in the following list:

ankle	heel
arm	hip
cheeks	knee
chest	leg
chin	lips
ears	mouth
elbow	neck
eyes	nose
face	shoulders
fingers	stomach
foot	thumb
hair	toes
hand	waist
head	wrist

exercise	1-4

Fill in the blanks.

1. The _____, _____, _____, _____, _____,

   _____, _____, _____, and _____ are on the *head*.

2. The *elbow* is in the middle of the _____.

3. The _____ is in the middle of the *leg*.

4. The _____ is between the *hand* and the *arm*.

5. The _____ is between the *foot* and the *leg*.

6. The *foot* has five _____; the *hand* has four _____ and one _____.

7. The *shoulders* are between the _____ and the _____.

8. The _____ is above the *stomach* and below the *chest*.

Words for Places

Outside Places

Review the words in the following list:

airport	gas station	railroad
apartment	grass	river
area	grocery store	road
bank	highway	school
barbershop	hill	shopping center
beach	hospital	shops
building	hotel	sidewalk
bus stop	house	street
church	land	suburb
city	library	sun
corner	moon	town
country	mountain	traffic light
drugstore	neighborhood	train station
farm	ocean	tree
florist	park	yard
garden	post office	

exercise 1-5

Circle the word that does not *belong in each group.*

1. airport — train station — road — bus stop

2. library — ocean — mountain — river

3. drugstore — grocery store — florist — sun

4. post office — bank — library — farm

5. street — highway — apartment — road

6. moon — house — hotel — apartment

7. tree — post office — yard — garden

8. church — highway — library — school

exercise	1-6

What places do you go to every day?

_____   _____

_____   _____

_____   _____

_____   _____

exercise	1-7

What places do you go to once or twice a week?

_____   _____

_____   _____

exercise	1-8

What places do you go to occasionally (sometimes)?

_____   _____

_____   _____

exercise	1-9

Where do you never go?

_____   _____

_____   _____

Inside Places

Review the words in the following list:

attic	front door
back door	hall
basement	kitchen
bathroom	laundry room
bedroom	library
ceiling	living room
classroom	office
corner	restaurant
department store	second floor
dining room	store
first floor	wall
floor	window

exercise   1-10

Write the name of the place or places where each of the following things is usually found.

1. bathtub _____

2. bed _____

3. bedspread _____

4. blackboard _____

5. blanket _____

6. book _____

7. bookshelf _____

8. buffet _____

9. bulletin board _____

10. chair _____

11. closet _____

12. coffeemaker _____

13. coffee table _____

14. computer _____

15. copier _____

16. counter   _____

17. cup   _____

18. desk   _____

19. detergent   _____

20. dish   _____

21. dishwasher   _____

22. dresser   _____

23. dryer   _____

24. elevator   _____

25. escalator   _____

26. facecloth   _____

27. fax machine   _____

28. filing cabinet   _____

29. fireplace   _____

30. fork   _____

31. garbage disposer   _____

32. glass   _____

33. knife   _____

34. lamp   _____

35. magazine   _____

36. microwave oven   _____

37. napkin   _____

38. newspaper   _____

39. night table   _____

40. notebook   _____

41. pan   _____

42. paper   _____

43. pen   _____

44. pencil   _____

45. pillow   _____

46. pillowcase   _____

47. plate   _____

48. printer   _____

49. refrigerator   _____

50. saucer   _____

51. sheet   _____

52. shower   _____

53. sink   _____

54. soap   _____

55. sofa   _____

56. spoon   _____

57. stairway   _____

58. stove   _____

59. table   _____

60. tea towel   _____

61. telephone   _____

62. toaster   _____

63. toilet   _____

64. towel   _____

65. TV set   _____

66. washing machine _____

Singular, Plural, and Noncount Nouns

Using Singular Nouns

English nouns can be divided into two categories: *count nouns* and *noncount nouns*.

A count noun is *singular* when there is *one* of the person, place, or thing it names.

When a noun is singular, use *a* or *an* before it. Use *a* if it begins with a *consonant* sound; use *an* if it begins with a *vowel* sound.

exercise	2-1

Write a *or* an *before each of the following singular nouns.*

1. _____ brother

2. _____ aunt

3. _____ artist

4. _____ employer

5. _____ janitor

6. _____ professor

7. _____ patient

8. _____ engineer

9. _____ reporter

10. _____ stewardess

11. _____ sister

12. _____ uncle

13. _____ dentist

14. _____ driver

15. _____ actor

16. _____ adviser

17. _____ accountant

18. _____ technician

19. _____ architect

20. _____ actress

21. _____ cheek

22. _____ chest

23. _____ leg

24. _____ ear

25. _____ mouth

26. _____ area

27. _____ apartment

28. _____ river

29. _____ bus stop

30. _____ basement

31. _____ elbow

32. _____ arm

33. _____ ankle

34. _____ nose

35. _____ eye

36. _____ library

37. _____ house

38. _____ ocean

39. _____ airport

40. _____ attic

Use *a* or *an* before a singular noun to answer the question *"What . . . ?"*

What do you do?	I'm **a** secretary. I'm **an** actor.
What is it?	It's **a** banana. It's **an** apple.
What do you want?	I want **a** house. I want **an** apartment.

Use the number *one* before a singular noun to answer the question *"How many . . . ?"*

How many cars do you have?	We have **one** car.
How many English classes are there?	There is **one** class.

Use *"There is . . ."* before a singular noun to indicate that it exists.

There is an accountant in my family.
There is a library on the corner.
There is only one bus stop on this street.

exercise	2-2

Look at page 13 of this book and answer the following questions. Be careful in your choice of a, an, *or* one *before each singular noun.*

1. What do you have in your hands?

   _____

2. What is there at the very end of this book?

   _____

3. In the word *Contents,* what is there between the first *n* and the *e?*

   _____

4. How many *e*'s are there in the word *Contents?*

   _____

Words for Groups of People

Some singular nouns name groups of people who have the same interest. These are called *collective* nouns. Use a collective noun with a singular verb form. Observe the following examples:

band	company
choir	family
chorus	government
class	orchestra
committee	team

exercise	2-3

Fill in each blank with a word from the previous list. Be sure to include a *or* an *in each blank before the noun.*

1. A group of people who take a course together is _____.

2. A group of people who play musical instruments together can be

   _____ or _____.

3. A group of people who form a business is _____.

4. People who are related by blood are _____.

5. A group of people who play together to win a game or sport is _____.

6. A group of people who control public policy in a country is _____.

7. A group of people who make plans for a larger group is called _____.

8. A group of people who sing together is _____ or

    _____.

Using Plural Nouns

A count noun is *plural* when there is *more than one* of the person, place, or thing it names. To make a singular noun plural:

- Add *-s*:

one tree	three tree**s**
one word	four word**s**
one sister	two sister**s**

- Add *-es* to a few words that end in *-o*:

one echo	two echo**es**
one mosquito	three mosquito**es**
one tomato	four tomato**es**
one hero	four hero**es**
one potato	two potato**es**
one tornado	two tornado**es**

- Add *-es* to nouns that end in *-ch*, *-sh*, *-ss*, and *-x*:

one beach	two beach**es**
one dish	four dish**es**
one dress	two dress**es**
one fax	three fax**es**

- Add *-ies* to nouns that end in a consonant followed by *-y*, after dropping the *-y*:

one city	two cit**ies**
one country	four countr**ies**
one family	two famil**ies**
one puppy	six pupp**ies**

- Add *-ves* to nouns that end in *-f* or *-fe*, after dropping the *-f* or *-fe*:

one calf	two cal**ves**
one half	two hal**ves**
one leaf	three lea**ves**
one knife	five kni**ves**

- Use an irregular form for certain nouns:

one child	two child**ren**
one man	four m**e**n
one person	three pe**ople**
one tooth	four t**ee**th
one mouse	three m**ice**
one woman	three w**ome**n
one foot	two f**ee**t

- Use the singular form for the plural for certain nouns:

one deer	three deer
one sheep	four sheep
one fish	two fish

exercise   **2-4**

Write the plural form of each of the following nouns.

1. brother _____

2. daughter _____

3. wife _____

4. baby _____

5. child _____

6. man _____

7. woman _____

8. teenager _____

9. artist _____

10. customer _____

11. student _____

12. actress _____

13. boss _____

14. nurse _____

15. eye _____

16. ear _____

17. toe _____

18. church _____

19. city _____

20. library _____

21. bus stop _____

22. post office _____

23. window _____

24. glass _____

25. knife   _____

26. fork   _____

27. stove   _____

28. facecloth   _____

exercise	2-5

Write the plural form of each of the following collective *nouns.*

1. band   _____

2. choir   _____

3. chorus   _____

4. class   _____

5. committee   _____

6. family   _____

7. government   _____

8. orchestra   _____

9. team   _____

Use *are there* and a plural noun in a question to ask if any exist and how many:

> **Are there any** cars in your driveway?
> How many cars **are there**?
> How many houses **are there** on this street?
> How many pages **are there** in this book?

Use *there are* followed by any number from *two* on up before a plural noun to tell how many of them exist:

> **There are two** cars in the driveway.
> **There are ten** houses on this street.
> **There are 208** pages in this book.

Use *there are* before the word *no* when it indicates *zero. No* is followed by a plural noun:

> **There are no** cars in the driveway.
> **There are no** houses on this street.

Not any can be used instead of *no* to indicate *zero*:

There are **not any** cars in the driveway.   There are**n't any** cars in the driveway.
There are **not any** houses on this street.   There are**n't any** houses on this street.

Words for Clothes and Accessories

Review the following examples:

For Men and Women	Usually for Women	Usually for Men
belt	blouse	necktie/bow tie
cap	bracelet	tuxedo
chain	dress	
coat	handbag/purse/pocketbook	
earring	necklace	
hat	nightgown	
jacket	skirt	
raincoat		
ring		
robe		
scarf		
shirt		
suit		
sweater		
sweatshirt		
T-shirt		
umbrella		
wallet		
watch		

exercise   2-6

Select twelve items from the preceding list, and write how many of each item there are in your closets and drawers.
Use There are *to begin each sentence.*

1. _____

2. _____

3. _____

4. _____

5. _____

6. _____

7. _____

8. _____

9. _____

10. _____

11. _____

12. _____

Pairs

Some clothing items are usually in two parts, which are sometimes separate, such as two *gloves*, and sometimes connected, such as *pants*. The nouns are plural. One set of two parts is a *pair*. A *pair of shoes*, for example, is two shoes, one for the left foot and one for the right. A *pair of pants* is one item, with two legs.

Review the following examples of *pairs*:

For Men and Women	Usually for Women
earrings	
glasses	
sunglasses	
gloves	
pajamas	
pants	
jeans	
shorts	
sweatpants	
shoes	
boots	flats
sandals	high heels
slippers	
socks	stockings
	tights

---

exercise   2-7

How many pairs *do you have in your closets and drawers?*

I have one pair of _____, one pair of _____, and one

pair of _____.

I have _____ pairs of _____,

_____ pairs of _____, and

_____ pairs of _____.

Quantities

To tell an approximate number of plural items there are, use:

some	=	more than one
a few	=	three or four
a lot of/ lots of/ many	=	a large number of/plenty of/enough
not many	=	a small number of
too many	=	more than is good or necessary

I have **some** tickets for the ball game.
There are **a few** seats in the front row.
A lot of people are going to the game.
There are **not many** seats.
There are **too many** people here.

exercise	2-8

Look at all of the lists of nouns for people, places, and things to answer the following questions.

1. What do you have *some* of? Begin each answer with *I have* . . .

_____

_____

_____

_____

_____

2. What are there *a lot of* outside? Begin each answer with *There are* . . .

_____

_____

_____

_____

_____

3. What are there *not many* of in the place where you live? Begin each answer with *There are* . . .

_____

_____

_____

_____

_____

4. What do you see *a few* of right now? Begin each answer with *I see* . . .

_____

_____

_____

_____

5. What do you have *too many* of? Begin each answer with *I have* . . .

_____

_____

_____

_____

Words for Food

Review the following words that name things to eat or drink. These nouns can be either singular or plural.

apple	nut
avocado	orange
banana	pea
bean	pear
carrot	potato
cherry	potato chip
doughnut	salad
drink	sandwich
egg	snack
grape	soda
hamburger	steak
hot dog	tomato
meal	vegetable

exercise	2-9

Write one of the following words or groups of words in each blank, depending on whether the nouns are singular or plural.

a   an   one   some   a lot of   a few   no   any   two

1. He eats _____ egg and _____ doughnut for breakfast.

2. I like to have _____ apple or _____ orange in the afternoon.

3. Would you like _____ peas and _____ carrots?

4. She wants _____ sandwich and _____ potato chips.

5. I want _____ banana.

6. We would like _____ hot dogs, please.

7. There aren't _____ hamburgers.

8. She is going to the store to buy _____ tomatoes.

9. She's going to buy _____ steaks for dinner.

10. I didn't order _____ salad; I ordered _____ vegetables instead.

Using Noncount Nouns

Many words for food are *noncount* nouns. Some examples are the words in the following list:

Liquids	Dry Items	Meat	Dairy Products	Vegetables	Other
beer	bread	bacon	butter	broccoli	cake
coffee	cereal	beef	cheese	cauliflower	candy
cream	flour	chicken	ice cream	corn	fruit
gravy	rice	fish	yogurt	eggplant	jam
juice	sugar	meat		lettuce	jelly
milk	toast	pork		spinach	pepper
sauce				squash	pie
soup					popcorn
tea					salt
water					
wine					

Many personal care items are also named by noncount nouns. Review the words in the following list:

aftershave lotion	lotion
bath gel	perfume
conditioner	shampoo
cream	shaving cream
fingernail polish	soap
fingernail polish remover	toothpaste

Use *is there any* before a noncount noun to ask if it exists:

> **Is there any** rice in the cupboard?
> **Is there any** fruit in the refrigerator?
> **Is there any** soap in the bathroom?

Use *how much* followed by a noncount noun plus *is there* to ask the amount of it that exists:

> **How much** ice cream **is there**?
> **How much** cereal **is there**?
> **How much** water **is there**?
> **How much** shampoo **is there**?

To tell the approximate amount of a noncount noun, use:

some	=	more than nothing
a lot of	=	a large amount of
a little	=	a small amount of
not much	=	a very small amount of
no/not any	=	nothing

> There is **some** ice cream in the freezer.
> There is **a lot of** fruit in the bowl.
> There is **a little** cereal in the box.
> There is **not much** shampoo.
> There is **no** water./There is**n't any** water.

exercise 2-10

Use words from the noncount noun food list to answer the following questions.

1. What is there a lot of in your refrigerator?

   _____

2. Is there any candy in the cupboard?

   _____

3. How much bread is there in the kitchen?

   _____

4. Is there any popcorn in the cupboard?

   _____

5. Is there too much of anything?

   _____

exercise	2-11

Use words from the noncount noun personal care items list to answer the following questions.

1. Is there any shampoo in your bathroom?

    _____

2. How much toothpaste is there?

    _____

3. What else is there?

    _____

To tell the exact amount of a noncount noun, use the singular or plural of the container of the item, the weight of the item, or the number of *pieces* or *servings* of it there are:

a can of soup	three cans of soup
a cup of coffee	two cups of coffee
a glass of milk	four glasses of milk
a bowl of cereal	a few bowls of cereal
one spoonful of sugar	two spoonfuls of sugar
one serving of spinach	three servings of spinach
a piece of meat	two pieces of meat
a tube of toothpaste	two tubes of toothpaste

Types of Containers	Weights and Measures	Serving Sizes
bag	cup	bite
bar	drop	piece
bottle	gallon	sip
bowl	ounce	slice
box	pint	
case	pound	
cup	quart	
glass	spoonful	
jar	tablespoon	
package	teaspoon	
plate		
tube		

exercise	2-12

Look at your answers to Exercise 2-10. Change the approximate amounts of each item to exact amounts and write the complete sentences here.

1. _____

2. _____

3. _____

4. _____

5. _____

exercise   2-13

Look at your answers to Exercise 2-11. Change the approximate amounts of each item to exact amounts and write the complete sentences here.

1. _____

2. _____

3. _____

exercise   2-14

Circle all of the words or sets of words that could be used in each blank.

1. There is _____ bread on the table.

   a little   a   a lot of   some   three slices of   no   a slice of

2. There are _____ bread on the table.

   a little   a few   some   three slices of   an   no

3. We need _____ ice cream.

   a little   some   three bowls of   many   a gallon of   two quarts of

4. She drank _____ milk.

   a glass of   three glasses of   a few   some   a little

5. They're going to buy _____ rice.

   some   a little   a few   two bags of   a   an   one

6. I would like to have _____ lettuce on my sandwich.

   a piece of   two pieces of   a little   a   two   some

7. He ate _____ cake.

   some   a piece of   piece of   two pieces of   three   a lot of

8. There is _____ pie in the refrigerator.

    some   a piece of   piece of   two pieces of   no   three

9. There are _____ cups of coffee here.

    a   two   one   a few   a little   some   no   any

10. I drink _____ juice every morning.

    a   two   a glass of   two glasses of   some   a lot of   too many

Words for Groups of Individual Items

Other *noncount* nouns include words that represent groups of individual items. The individual items can be counted, but the word that represents the entire group cannot.

Furniture	Mail	Jewelry	Money	Information	Trash
bed	advertisement	bracelet	dime	brochure	boxes
chair	bill	earrings	dollar bill	notice	packaging
desk	letter	necklace	five	pamphlet	used items
dresser	postcard	pin	nickel	report	
nightstand	penny				
sofa	quarter				
table	ten				
	twenty				

For a Desk	For Cooking	Hardware	Medicine	Makeup	Entertainment
paper	pan	hammer	capsule	blush	game
pen	pot	nail	drop	eyebrow pencil	movie
pencil	spatula	pliers	pill	foundation	party
scissors	spoon	screw	tablet	lipstick	radio
tape		screwdriver		mascara	show
		wrench		powder	television

There is *some* furniture.   There are three chairs.
You have *a little* mail.   You have two letters and a postcard.
She has *a lot of* jewelry.   She has five necklaces, four bracelets, and
                                            twenty pairs of earrings.

He has *a little* money.   He has a ten, a five, and three quarters.
We got *some* information.   We got a brochure and two reports.
There is *too much* trash.   There are boxes, old clothes, broken toys,
                                            worn-out tires, and broken dishes.

exercise	2-15

Answer each question.

1. How much furniture do you have?

   _____

2. What mail do you usually receive?

   _____

3. What jewelry do you like to wear?

   _____

4. How much money do you have in your pocket?

   _____

5. What do you throw in the trash every day?

   _____

There are many things that cannot be counted. Like all noncount nouns, words for these things do not have plural forms. Review the words in the following list:

advice	help	poverty
air	homework	rain
beauty	housework	sickness
cold	intelligence	snow
courage	kindness	strength
darkness	light	water
health	news	wealth
heat	pollution	work

There is some housework to do.
There is a lot of news.
There is a little snow in the mountains.
There is not much heat in the house.
There is too much rain.

Do *not* use *a, an, one, many,* or any number with a noncount noun.

exercise	2-16

Circle all of the words that can be used in each blank space.

1. We have _____ help.

   many   **a little**   **four**   **an**

2. There is _____ heat.

   no   **too many**   **some**   **a little**

3. They need _____ advice.

   some   **an**   **not many**   **a lot of**

4. She has _____ work.

   many   **some**   **a little**   **a**   **an**

5. There is _____ poverty in the city.

   a   **too much**   **not many**   **a lot of**

| **exercise** | **2-17** |

Answer the following questions. Use no, not much, some, a little, a lot of, *or* too much *before each noncount noun.*

1. Do you have news about your friends in your country? Begin your answer with *I have* . . .

   _____

2. Is there work available in this city? Begin your answer with *There is* . . .

   _____

3. How much rain is there here in the summer? Begin your answer with *There is* . . .

   _____

4. Do you need advice? Begin your answer with *I need* . . .

   _____

5. Is there pollution in your area? Begin your answer with *There is* . . .

   _____

Using Articles with Singular, Plural, and Noncount Nouns

The indefinite articles *a* and *an* are used before singular nouns that refer to any one of that person, place, or thing:

> **A** clock is **an** instrument that marks time.
> **A** watch is **a** clock that you wear on your wrist.

The previous sentences do not name a specific clock or watch; they refer to clocks and watches in general.

The articles *a* and *an* can refer to a specific singular noun to tell or ask someone about it for the first time:

I have **a** clock that is 150 years old.
Her boyfriend gave her **a** watch for her birthday.

There are no indefinite articles for plural and noncount nouns. To refer to people, places, or things in general, *no* word (Ø) is placed before the plural or noncount noun:

Ø Clocks are instruments that mark time.
Ø Mail includes anything that can be delivered by the post office.

No word (Ø) can refer to a plural or noncount noun to tell or ask someone about it for the first time:

Her boyfriend brings her Ø flowers every week.
You got Ø mail this morning.

exercise   2-18

Fill in each blank with one of the following.

 a   an   Ø

1. I am going to buy _____ orange.

2. They sell _____ oranges at the market on the corner.

3. Do you have _____ fruit?

4. Yes, we have _____ oranges and _____ apples.

5. Where do they sell _____ furniture in this city?

6. I'm looking for _____ table, _____ chairs, and _____ desk.

7. We need _____ information.

8. Can you give me _____ advice?

9. Do you have _____ kitchen equipment?

10. I want to buy _____ pot and _____ frying pan.

The definite article *the* is used before a singular noun, a plural noun, or a noncount noun to refer to a specific person, place, or thing.

The is used when the speaker and the listener both know which particular item is being referred to:

She showed me **the** watch *her boyfriend gave her* for her birthday.
The flowers *he sent her* were beautiful.
The furniture *I bought* was cheap.

exercise	2-19

Fill in each blank with one of the following:

        a   **an**   **Ø**   **the**

1. I bought _____ radio yesterday.

2. Where is _____ radio (you bought)?

3. We have _____ kitchen equipment on sale.

4. Where is _____ kitchen equipment (that you have on sale)?

5. I love _____ flowers.

6. Are these _____ flowers your friend sent you?

7. Where is _____ medicine the doctor gave you?

8. Are these _____ pills you are taking?

9. He is looking for _____ information.

10. He didn't like _____ information he got from the company.

exercise	2-20

Write two sentences that tell about one thing you have. Use a *or* an *in the first sentence to introduce it. Use* the *in the second sentence to tell more about it.*

1. _____

2. _____

_____

exercise	2-21

Write two sentences that tell about something you have more than one of. Use Ø *in the first sentence to introduce the items. Use* the *in the second sentence to tell more about them.*

1. _____

2. _____

_____

exercise **2-22**

Write two sentences that tell about a noncount item you have. Use Ø in the first sentence to introduce it. Use the in the second sentence to tell more about it.

1. _____

2. _____

_____

The is used when there is only one possible reference:

> I left my keys in **the** car. (the car I drive)
> Please put the bags in **the** kitchen. (the only kitchen in the house)
> Please feed **the** dog. (the dog we own)

exercise **2-23**

Fill in each blank with one of the following:

a	an	the	Ø

1. We bought _____ car last night.

2. _____ cars are expensive.

3. _____ car we bought is a convertible.

4. Do you like _____ convertibles?

5. Do you like _____ convertible we bought?

Using Demonstrative Pronouns with Singular, Plural, and Noncount Nouns

There are four *demonstrative pronouns*: *this, that, these,* and *those. This* and *these* refer to nouns that are close enough to touch, things that are *here.*

Use *this* before a singular or noncount noun; use *these* before a plural noun:

> **This** watch is the one I like.
> **These** watches are very expensive.
> **This** jewelry is very expensive.

That and *those* refer to nouns that are not close enough to touch, things that are *there*:

> Do you like **that** dress in the store window?
> **Those** dresses in front are very pretty.
> **That** information about the prices is not correct.

exercise	2-24

Fill in each blank with this, that, these, *or* those.

1. _____ book in my hands is very interesting.

2. What are _____ things he is carrying?

3. We're going to see _____ new movie at the Odeon.

4. Come here and look at _____ pictures with me.

5. Who is _____ girl over there?

6. Who are _____ girls over there?

7. Hi, I'm Sally and _____ are my friends, Amy and Courtney.

8. I'm wearing _____ sweater because I'm cold.

Proper Nouns

A *proper noun* is the name that has been given to a person, a group of people, a place, or a thing. The names of religions and of languages are proper nouns. A proper noun is written with a capital letter at the beginning of each word. Here are some examples of proper nouns:

Betty	Garden Club
John Clark	Planning Committee
Capitol Hill	February
Oak Street	French
Monday	Ireland
The Daily Mirror	

Longer names and titles of books often have prepositions and articles, which are not written with capital letters, except when those words appear at the beginning:

The University of the East   *A Boy's Life in the Country*

 exercise   3-1

Change lowercase letters to capital letters where necessary.

1. She's reading a book called *a guide to good manners.*

2. We have to go to the springfield library on monday.

3. They are from italy, and they don't speak spanish.

4. david is going to go to wilson academy for boys in september.

exercise	3-2

Write the proper names of people, places, or things you know.

1. A person I know: _____

2. The street I live on: _____

3. The name of a school: _____

4. The language I speak: _____

5. The country I'm from: _____

6. A river in my country: _____

7. A newspaper: _____

8. A book I like: _____

9. Today's day: _____

10. The date of my birthday: _____

11. A group I belong to: _____

12. A restaurant I like: _____

Possessive Nouns and Pronouns

Possessive Nouns

A *possessive noun* indicates that the person, place, or thing named is the owner or holder of the noun that follows. It answers the question *Whose . . . ?* A possessive noun can be used before a singular noun, a plural noun, or a noncount noun.

It can be a proper noun followed by *-'s*:

    Emily's dress   **Bill's** shoes.   **Susan's** ice cream

A possessive noun can be a common noun followed by *-'s*:

    the **teacher's** desk   the **man's** glasses   a **friend's** mail

When two or more people own or have something, the plural noun is followed by an apostrophe if it ends in *-s*:

    the **teachers'** party the **students'** books   my **friends'** health

If the plural form does not end in *-s*, it is followed by *-'s*:

    the **men's** cars   the **children's** class   the **people's** money

exercise	4-1

Write a phrase with a possessive noun for each item listed.

1. car/my sister _____

2. hats/the men _____

3. party/the children _____

4. office/the doctor _____

5. apartment/the girls _____

6. class/Miss Smith _____

7. school/Ben Lindsay _____

8. meeting/the ladies _____

exercise	4-2

Look at some photographs of your family and friends. Write five things you see, and indicate to whom they belong.

EXAMPLES: That's Debbie's dog.
Those are my sister's shoes.

1. _____

2. _____

3. _____

4. _____

5. _____

Possessive Pronouns

A *possessive pronoun* can be used in place of a possessive noun. A possessive pronoun can be used before a singular, plural, or noncount noun. These are the possessive pronouns:

my	it belongs to **me**
your	it belongs to **you**
his	it belongs to **him**
her	it belongs to **her**
its	it belongs to **an animal, a group, or an organization**
our	it belongs to **me and one or more other people**
your	it belongs to **you and one or more other people**
their	it belongs to **one or more other people, animals, groups, or organizations**

I drive **my** car to work.
Do you have **your** driver's license?
Bob gave me **his** telephone number.   He gave me **his** telephone number.
Jane doesn't have **her** ticket.   She doesn't have **her** ticket.
Susan and I bought **our** supplies.   We bought **our** supplies.
Do you and Sam have **your** books?   Do you have **your** books?

exercise	4-3

Look at your answers to Exercise 4-1. Change the possessive nouns to possessive pronouns.

1. _____

2. _____

3. _____

4. _____

5. _____

6. _____

7. _____

8. _____

exercise	4-4

Look at your answers to Exercise 4-2. Change the possessive nouns to possessive pronouns.

1. _____

2. _____

3. _____

4. _____

5. _____

Review of Singular, Plural, and Noncount Nouns

These are similarities between *singular, plural,* and *noncount* nouns:

- All can follow *the*:

    the letter   **the** letters   **the** mail

- All can follow a *possessive noun*:

    John's letter   **John's** letters   **John's** mail

- All can follow a *possessive pronoun*:

    his letter   **his** letters   **his** mail

These are similarities between *singular* and *noncount* nouns:

- Both can follow *this*:

    this letter   **this** mail

- Both are followed by *a singular verb*:

    The letter **is** here.   The mail **is** here.

These are similarities between *plural* and *noncount* nouns:

- They can follow *no*:

    no letters   **no** mail

- They can follow *not any*:

    not any letters   **not any** mail

- They can follow *some*:

    some letters   **some** mail

- They can follow *a lot of* or *lots of*:

      a lot of letters   **a lot of** mail
      lots of letters   **lots of** mail

- They can be used with no word (Ø) before them, to make a general statement:

      Ø Letters are stamped at the post office.
      Ø Mail is stamped at the post office.

These are characteristics of *singular* nouns only:

- They can follow *a* or *an*:

      a banana   **an** orange

These are characteristics of *plural* nouns only:

- They can follow *a few*:

      a few bananas   **a few** letters

- They can follow *not many* or *too many*:

      not many bananas   **too many** letters

These are characteristics of *noncount* nouns only:

- They can follow *a little*:

      a little fruit   **a little** mail

- They can follow *not much* or *too much*:

      not much fruit   **too much** mail

exercise	5-1

Circle the word that correctly fills in each blank.

1. There are _____ people in this room.

   a   **one**   **too many**   **too much**

2. There is _____ artist in our family.

   a   **some**   **a lot of**   **an**   **these**

3. Do you have _____ books I gave you?

   a   **too many**   **the**   **too much**   **an**

4. _____ airplanes are making a lot of noise.

   Too much   **Ø**   **Those**   **This**   **A little**

5. I'm hoping you can give me _____ advice.

   too many   **an**   **one**   **three**   **a little**

6. Our neighbors have _____ children.

   too much   **a lot of**   **a little**   **one**   **a**

7. The doctor says that I eat _____ salt.

   too many   **a few**   **a**   **too much**   **this**

8. There are _____ tickets available.

   too much   **this**   **that**   **no**   **a little**

9. _____ apartment is near my house.

   John's   **A few**   **A lot of**   **Some**   **A**

10. We would like _____ help.

    some   **a few**   **a**   **many**   **one**

exercise   5-2

Match the words in the left column with the nouns in the right column.

1. one   bottles
   four   bottle

2. these   information
   that   letters

3. a few   pills
   a little   medicine

4. too much   sugar
   one   spoonfuls
   a few   spoonful

5. too many   furniture
   not much   chairs
   a   chair

6. a   jewelry
   these   necklace
   a little   earrings

7. that   vegetables
   those   fruit

8. There is a   hardware
   There are   nail
   There is   screws

9. There is one   water
   There are no   lights
   There is no   lamp

10. Here is your   letters
    There are no   letter

Verbs Used as Nouns

The *present participle* form of a verb can be used as a noun to be the subject of a sentence, or the object of a verb or a preposition. Present participles are called *gerunds* when they are used as nouns. (See page 96 for the formation of *present participles.*)

Gerund as Subject	Gerund as Object
Walking is good exercise.	We enjoy **walking**.
Eating well is important.	I like **eating** at this restaurant.
Working here is interesting.	She is tired of **working** here.
Playing with other children makes her happy.	He talks about **playing** with other children.

exercise 6-1

Fill in each blank with the gerund *form of the verb indicated.*

1. We are very tired of (wait) _____ for her.

2. (drive) _____ at night can be dangerous.

3. Do you like (live) _____ here?

4. They argued about her (cook) _____.

5. (study) _____ at the university gave him a good background.

6. We're not afraid of (stay) _____ alone.

exercise   6-2

Write sentences that change the verbs to nouns.

1. sing ——————————————————————————————

2. drink ——————————————————————————————

3. sleep ——————————————————————————————

4. write ——————————————————————————————

5. study ——————————————————————————————

More Specific Nouns

There are many nouns that can replace general nouns to describe specific people, places, things, and ideas. Some examples follow. *Formal* indicates that the word is used mainly in writing. *Informal* indicates that the word is used mainly in conversation. *Slang* indicates that the word is very informal and that it is currently in style.

Words for People

boy: *a male child from birth to age eighteen*
My sister has three children, two **boys** and a girl.

bum: *a person who makes no effort to succeed*
She says her neighbor is a lazy **bum**.

dude: *a man who pays a lot of attention to his clothes*
Her new boyfriend is a handsome **dude**.

    form of address to a friend (slang)
    "**Dude**, we're having a party; come on over."

    a stranger (slang)
    I was walking down the street and that **dude** started talking to me.

gentleman: *a man with good manners*
Your brother is a perfect **gentleman**.

girl: *a female child from birth to age eighteen*
Your daughter is a lovely **girl**.

    a young, unmarried woman
    Our neighbor is a **girl** who is in law school.

guy: *a boy or man (informal)*
That **guy** who works at the drugstore is very helpful.

kid: *a male or female child (informal)*
> There are a lot of **kids** in that family.

lady: *a woman with good manners*
> The **lady** who lives across the street is a teacher.

man: *an adult male*
> There are six **men** in the study group.

tomboy: *a girl who likes to play boys' games*
> When I was ten years old I was a real **tomboy**.

woman: *an adult female*
> I met an interesting **woman** at the meeting.

young lady: *a young woman with good manners*
> The girls have grown up and are now charming **young ladies**.

youth: *a young man*
> One of the **youths** at the convention gave a good speech.

young people
> The **youth** of today have many opportunities.

exercise 7-1

Replace each italicized word with a more descriptive one from the previous list.

1. How many *children* does she have? _____

2. Did you notice the *boy* in the yellow shirt? _____

3. My brother's new girlfriend is an accomplished *girl*. _____

4. I don't want to be a *lazy person* who has no ambition. _____

Friends

acquaintance: *a person you have met but don't know very well*
> An **acquaintance** of mine works in your office.

boyfriend: *a male who is someone's romantic interest*
> Are you bringing your **boyfriend** to the party?

classmate: *a person who is in the same class with someone at school*
> The school is so big, I don't even know all of my **classmates**.

colleague: *a person someone works with professionally*
> All of my **colleagues** agree with the new plan.

companion: *a friend someone spends a lot of time with or lives with*
> They are good **companions**; they go everywhere together.

coworker: *a person who works in the same place as someone*
> She cannot get along with any of her **coworkers**.

fiancé: *a male to whom someone is engaged to be married*
He gave her a diamond ring, so now he's her **fiancé**.

fiancée: *a female to whom someone is engaged to be married*
She has been his **fiancée** for five years.

friend: *a person you know and like*
She has a lot of **friends** here.

girfriend: *a female who is someone's romantic interest*
I can't bring my **girlfriend**, because she lives in another city.

partner: *a companion*
Her **partner** works at the local nursery.

a person who co-owns a business with someone
My doctor is out of town, but his **partner** will see me.

roommate: *a person someone shares a room with*
We have a big room at college, so I have two **roommates**.

exercise 7-2

Fill in each blank with the most appropriate word from the previous list.

1. My aunt got engaged last month, and she is coming to visit with her new _____.

2. Her daughter, who is in college, complains that her _____ doesn't help clean the bathroom.

3. I don't like the boss's new program, but my _____ think it will work.

4. He's not a good friend of mine, just an _____.

Doctors

dentist: *a doctor who takes care of the teeth*
It's a good idea to see a **dentist** at least once a year.

dermatologist: *a skin specialist*
A **dermatologist** can help you with your allergies.

doctor/M.D.: *a person who has the degree of Doctor of Medicine, works to help sick people, and is licensed to prescribe medicine*
When you are sick, you should go to the **doctor**.

ear, nose, and throat doctor/E.N.T.: *a specialist for the ear, the nose, and the throat*
She sees an **E.N.T.** for her sinusitis.

eye doctor/ophthalmologist: *a specialist for eyes*
The **ophthalmologist** prescribed glasses for our son.

gastroenterologist: *a stomach specialist*
He is seeing a **gastroenterologist** to help cure his digestive problems.

general practitioner/G.P.: *an M.D. who treats most common diseases and ailments*
>   Our **G.P.** takes care of the whole family in one visit.

gynecologist: *a specialist in women's health*
>   Many women are checked by a **gynecologist** once a year.

obstetrician: *a specialist in the delivery of babies*
>   As soon as she suspected she was pregnant, she went to see an **obstetrician**.

orthodontist: *a dentist who specializes in straightening teeth*
>   The **orthodontist** fixed her crooked teeth, and now she has a beautiful smile.

orthopedist: *a specialist in bones*
>   When he broke his leg, the **orthopedist** put it in a cast.

pediatrician: *a specialist in children's health*
>   As soon as the baby was born he was examined by a **pediatrician**.

periodontist: *a dentist who specializes in gums*
>   The **periodontist** was able to help prevent gum recession in most patients.

podiatrist: *a specialist in feet*
>   The **podiatrist** told her not to wear high-heeled shoes.

specialist: *an M.D. who is an expert in one type of disease or part of the body*
>   Our G.P. recommended that we take our child to a **specialist**.

surgeon: *a specialist who performs major operations*
>   The **surgeon** was in the operating room for four hours.

exercise   7-3

Match the health problem in the left column to the doctor in the right column. (Note: there are more problems than types of doctor.)

_____ 1. a woman thinks she is pregnant   a. dentist

_____ 2. a baby cries for three days   b. dermatologist

_____ 3. a child has red spots on his legs   c. pediatrician

_____ 4. a girl breaks her arm   d. eye doctor

_____ 5. a man needs glasses   e. obstetrician

_____ 6. a boy has earaches   f. E.N.T. doctor

_____ 7. a woman has a bad cold   g. G.P.

_____ 8. a girl's skin itches   h. orthopedist

_____ 9. a woman has a toothache   i. orthodontist

_____ 10. a girl needs braces for her teeth

Artists

actor: *a male artist who performs in the theater, on television, or in the movies*
Which **actor** plays the main character in that film?

actress: *a female artist who performs in the theater, on television, or in the movies*
She is an **actress** who is able to play many different roles.

artist: *a person who works in a creative way*
The **artist** captured the beauty of the landscape.

designer: *an artist who works in clothing or home fashion*
She wears dresses only by her favorite **designer**.

musician: *an artist who composes or performs music*
He is an accomplished **musician** who writes all the songs he sings.

painter: *an artist who makes pictures with oil, watercolor, or another color medium*
The president's portrait was done by a famous **painter**.

photographer: *an artist who works with a camera to depict images*
We need a good **photographer** to capture the emotion of the celebration.

poet: *an artist who writes lyrical verses*
The **poet**'s words made me feel both happy and sad.

sculptor: *an artist who carves or models figures*
This **sculptor** prefers to work with marble.

writer: *an artist who puts words on paper to describe or narrate*
My favorite **writer** makes me feel that I am in the place he is describing.

exercise	7-4

Write the names of five artists you like, indicating the specific work of each one.

1. _____

2. _____

3. _____

4. _____

5. _____

Musicians

Review the words for musicians who play individual instruments:

cello	cellist
clarinet	clarinetist
drums	drummer
guitar	guitarist
keyboard	keyboardist
piano	pianist
saxophone	saxophonist
trombone	trombonist
trumpet	trumpeter
violin	violinist

Review more words for people involved in music:

alto	a female singer with a low voice
bass	a male singer with a low voice
choir or chorus director	someone who directs a group of singers
conductor	someone who directs a band or an orchestra
singer	a person who makes music with his or her voice
soprano	a female singer with a high voice
tenor	a male singer with a high voice

exercise   7-5

Write the names of five musicians you like, indicating the specialty of each one.

1. _____

2. _____

3. _____

4. _____

5. _____

Words for the Arts

Music

blues: *a style of slow jazz evolved from African-American songs*
I love to listen to the **blues** when I'm lonely.

classical: *European music of the latter half of the eighteenth century; music of acknowledged excellence and serious style*
Classical music is often performed by the city's symphony orchestra.

country: *a style of popular music from the rural American south and southwest*
A lot of **country** musicians live and work in Nashville, Tennessee.

folk/ethnic: *music that originates among the common people of a region*
Folk music was very popular in the United States in the 1960s.

jazz: *a kind of music that originated with African-American bands in the southern United States, characterized by improvisation and strong, flexible rhythm*
Jazz is popular in many parts of the world.

oldies: *popular music from an earlier decade*
Her favorite **oldies** are from the 1950s and 1960s.

popular: *music that is appreciated by a large number of people during the current period of time*
That radio station plays only **popular** music.

rap: *a currently popular style of music that originated among African-American performers, characterized by talking, rather than singing, in rhyme and rhythm*
Rap is for listening, not dancing.

rhythm and blues: *a style of music with strong, simple rhythm and lyrics that originated in the late 1940s and early 1950s among African-American groups*
Rhythm and blues is great for swing dancing.

rock: *a popular style of music played by bands with electric guitars, keyboards, and drums, often with emotional singing by a group or one singer*
Rock concerts are very popular among young people.

rock and roll: *a style of music that began in the 1950s and combined elements of rhythm and blues and country*
There were a lot of TV shows with **rock-and-roll** dancers.

exercise   7-6

Which of these types of music do you like best? Write a few sentences to describe the music and the musicians who play it.

_____

_____

_____

Dance

ballet: *a formal, artistic dance with graceful movements and elaborate technique*
> She has been dancing **ballet** since she was a child.

> *a ballet show*
>> We went to the **ballet** last night.

ballroom: *a formal version of popular dance, where style and technique are important, including the* fox-trot, waltz, swing, *and* Latin, *among others*
> I'm learning the waltz from my neighbor who teaches **ballroom** dancing.

dance: *movement in time with music*
> **Dance** is a good way to exercise and relax at the same time.

> *an event where people go to dance*
>> Are you going to the **dance** on Saturday night?

jazz: *a type of ballet performed to jazz music*
> She is a top ballet performer and is also accomplished in **jazz**.

Latin: *any of the dances performed to popular music from Latin America, including* merengue, salsa, cumbia, bachata, mambo, samba, cha-cha, *and* tango, *among others*
> He is a good swing dancer, but what he really likes is **Latin** dancing.

line: *a dance performed to country music, where dancers dance individually but all follow the same steps*
> One good thing about **line** dancing is that you don't need a partner.

tap: *a dance performed with a metal plate attached to the toe or heel of the shoe*
> She is good at both ballet and **tap**.

---

exercise | 7-7

Write a sentence that tells what kind of dance you have seen or have performed.

_____

_____

Words for Places

Parks

amusement park: *a park operated as a business that has rides, games, and other entertainment*
> All of the children wanted to go on the rides at the **amusement park**.

botanical garden: *a park where plants are cultivated and identified for the public*
> There was a beautiful display of orchids at the **botanical garden**.

national or state park: *a parcel of land reserved by the government and administered by the government for preservation and recreation*
> You can get a lot of information from the government about visiting the **national parks**.

park: *an outdoor place reserved for the pleasure of the public*
> We had a picnic in the **park**.

playground: *a park set aside for children to play in, usually with swings and other equipment for them to play on*

The kids were tired after an afternoon at the **playground**.

theme park: *an elaborate amusement park that is developed around one particular idea, such as a historical time or place, a popular character, or other special interest*

We saw a lot of movie and TV characters at the **theme park**.

zoo: *a park where animals are kept and shown to the public*

The children loved seeing the giraffes at the **zoo**.

| exercise | 7-8 |

Match each type of park in the left column with its description in the right column.

_____ 1. amusement park   a. a large park with people dressed in special costumes

_____ 2. botanical garden   b. a small park with swings and a sandbox

_____ 3. national park   c. a park with elephants, monkeys, lions, and tigers

_____ 4. playground   d. a park where you pay to go on rides

_____ 5. theme park   e. a large park that preserves the natural environment

_____ 6. zoo   f. a park where you can learn about different varieties of plants

Stores

boutique: *a small specialty store that sells goods carefully chosen for a particular type of customer and usually offers unique items that are not available at chain stores*

Her sister has individual style and shops only at **boutiques**.

box store: *a large chain store that has a similar structure and layout in each location*

If you need hardware for a project, you can go to a local hardware store or to a big **box store**.

chain store: *one of many stores owned and operated by the same company*

With so many **chain stores**, our cities are becoming more alike.

department store: *a large store that usually has several floors, elevators and escalators, and separate departments for each type of purchase—for example, women's clothing, men's clothing, children's clothing, shoes, linens, kitchen equipment, etc.*

It is very convenient to shop at a **department store** where you can find things for the whole family as well as household goods.

discount store: *a store that sells goods at a lower price than the one suggested by the manufacturer*

You can save a lot of money by buying at a **discount store**, but you don't get any help in selecting your purchases.

mall store: *a chain store often located with other chain stores in a shopping mall*

My friend loves to shop at her favorite **mall stores**.

outlet: *a store that sells goods from a particular manufacturer, at a lower price*

Outlets are often grouped together in malls on the outskirts of cities.

exercise   **7-9**

Write the name of a store you know that fits each category listed.

1. chain store   _____

2. box store   _____

3. department store   _____

4. discount store   _____

5. outlet   _____

6. mall store   _____

7. boutique   _____

Schools

academy: *a private school*
> He was educated at a very expensive **academy**.

college: *education beyond high school, where students take general required courses and specialize in a particular area of study leading to a bachelor's degree*
> Her mother made sure that she would be able to go to **college**.

elementary school: *a school that contains classes from kindergarten through grade five or six*
> Most children go to an **elementary school** near where they live.

graduate school: *the university programs that lead to advanced degrees, including special schools such as law school, medical school, dental school, and business school*
> Many students have full-time jobs and go to **graduate school** classes in the evening.

high school: *a school that contains classes from grades nine or ten through twelve*
> Graduation from **high school** is a requirement for admission to a college or university, and for many jobs.

kindergarten: *the first year of school, required in the United States by children aged five*
> Many children learn to read in **kindergarten**.

middle school: *a school that contains classes from grade six or seven to grade eight or nine*
> **Middle school** students are usually in the beginning stages of adolescence.

preschool: *a school for children aged three or four*
> **Preschool** is a good introduction to school for small children.

private school: *a school administered by a private organization, business, church, or other group*
> Most **private schools** require the students to wear uniforms.

public school: *a school administered by a local government where instruction is free*
> All of their children go to **public school**.

school: *a place for learning*
> He is going to open a cooking **school** in the city.

university: *a college that has four-year bachelor's degree programs and also offers graduate programs where students can do more in-depth study of a chosen subject, leading to a master's degree or a doctor's degree*
Some students prefer to get a bachelor's degree from a small college and then go to a large **university** for a master's degree.

exercise	7-10

Match each type of school with the students who would most likely attend it.

_____ 1. college   a. a three-year-old child

_____ 2. elementary school   b. a nine-year-old child

_____ 3. graduate school   c. the majority of children in the United States

_____ 4. high school   d. a five-year-old child

_____ 5. kindergarten   e. a twelve-year-old child

_____ 6. language school   f. a sixteen-year-old

_____ 7. middle school   g. a person who wants to continue to study after high school

_____ 8. preschool   h. a person who wants to continue to study after college

_____ 9. public school   j. a person who wants to learn French

Words for Things

Houses

apartment: *a place to live that is part of a larger building, owned by a landlord who collects monthly rent*
They will rent an **apartment** until they have enough money to buy a house.

cabin: *a small, roughly built house*
The family likes to stay in a **cabin** in the mountains in the summer.

a bedroom on a ship
The **cabins** on the ship are quite small.

an inside area of an airplane
Those airplanes have a very large passenger **cabin**.

condominium: *a building or group of buildings whose apartments are individually owned*
They are building a new **condominium** near here.

an apartment in a condominium
As soon as he graduated he bought a **condominium** in the city.

cottage: *a small house of one story*
His family has a **cottage** at the beach, where they go every summer.

house: *a building designed as a place to live*
>They are expecting a baby and want to move to a bigger **house**.

hut: *a small shelter, with no amenities*
>The children made a **hut** in the woods.

mansion: *a large house*
>The mayor's official residence is a beautiful **mansion**.

rambler: *a house, bigger than a cottage, that has a number of rooms that are all on one floor.*
>They are looking for a **rambler**, because her mother can't climb steps.

townhouse: *a house built in a row of houses, with side walls connected*
>**Townhouses** usually have a lot of steps.

exercise   7-11

Match each type of home in the column on the left with its description from the column on the right.

_____ 1. hut

_____ 2. cabin

_____ 3. condominium

_____ 4. cottage

_____ 5. apartment

_____ 6. mansion

_____ 7. rambler

_____ 8. townhouse

a. one bedroom, one bath, living room, dining room, kitchen, in a large building of similar units all owned by a company

b. one bedroom, one bath, living room, dining room, kitchen, in a large building of similar units each individually owned

c. living room, dining room, kitchen on main level, two bedrooms and bath on second level, one bedroom and bath on third level, recreation room in basement, in row of similar houses

d. seven bedrooms, eight bathrooms, twelve-foot ceilings, ballroom, swimming pool, guest house, on two landscaped acres

e. one room, mud floor, low ceiling

f. bedroom–living room combination, kitchen, outdoor shower, toilet in outhouse

g. five bedrooms, four bathrooms, living room, dining room, kitchen, all on one floor

h. two bedrooms, kitchen–dining room combination, living room, one bath, all on one floor, pretty rose garden and white picket fence

Streets

avenue: *a wide street in a city*
>The **avenues** in the city are wide and elegant.

beltway: *a freeway that forms a circle around a city, connecting its outer suburbs*
>Traffic is fast on the **beltway**, and you have to be careful.

freeway: *a highway with several lanes and few or no stoplights; vehicles enter and exit via ramps*
>There are always a lot of trucks on the **freeway**.

highway: *a main public road that connects towns and cities*
The **highway** is usually crowded.

road: *an open way for the passage of vehicles, people, or animals*
The **road** that leads to our cabin is not paved.

street: *a public way for automobiles, usually with buildings on both sides*
What **street** do you live on?

toll road: *a freeway that charges money to use it*
We took the **toll road** and got there much faster, but it cost ten dollars in tolls.

---

exercise   7-12

Write the names or route numbers of examples of each type of street.

1. street   _____

2. road   _____

3. avenue   _____

4. highway   _____

5. freeway   _____

6. toll road   _____

7. beltway   _____

Automobiles

automobile: *a passenger vehicle that has four wheels and its own engine, for travel on land*
Many families have more than one **automobile**.

car: *an automobile*
Our neighbors just bought a new **car**.

convertible: *a car whose top can be folded back or removed*
It's very pleasant to ride in a **convertible** in nice weather.

sedan: *a car that has a front seat and a rear seat and either two doors or four doors*
The **sedan** is a popular car style.

SUV: *(Sport Utility Vehicle) a high-performance four-wheel-drive car built on a truck frame*
There are lots of **SUVs** on the streets, especially in the suburbs.

van: *a large boxlike automobile that has sliding side doors*
Many people who have small children buy either an SUV or a **van**.

vehicle: *any device used for carrying passengers, goods, or equipment*
Bicycles, motorcycles, cars, and sleds are all **vehicles**.

exercise   7-13

Observe on the street examples of each type of vehicle listed, and make a note of the name of each one. Write a description of the color and make of each one.

1. sedan _____

2. convertible _____

3. SUV _____

4. van _____

Shoes

boots: *a protective covering for the feet and part of the legs*
   You need **boots** for walking in the snow.

flats: *women's shoes that have a very low heel*
   Flats are more comfortable for walking.

high heels: *women's shoes that have a built-up heel, often three to four inches high*
   Many women like to get dressed up in **high heels**.

lace-ups: *shoes that are tightened to the feet by laces that are threaded through holes in the upper part of the shoe*
   Children usually get their first **lace-ups** when they are learning to walk.

loafers: *men's or women's slip-on leather shoes that look like moccasins with a solid sole*
   Loafers are more casual than oxfords, but they are dressier than sneakers.

Mary Janes: *little girls' shoes with a strap over the top*
   Even big girls and women like **Mary Janes**.

moccasins: *soft leather shoes traditionally worn by native North Americans*
   Mocassins are especially pretty when they have decorative beading.

oxfords: *leather lace-ups*
   Some private schools require the students to wear **oxfords** as part of the school uniform.

pumps: *women's medium-heel or high-heel shoes with closed toe*
   Pumps can be worn almost anywhere.

sandals: *shoes made of a sole and straps*
   Sandals are great in the summertime.

shoes: *a covering for a person's feet*
   Everybody likes to get new **shoes**.

sneakers: *sports shoes with rubber soles; tennis shoes, running shoes, basketball shoes, etc.*
   People of all ages wear **sneakers**.

wedges: *high heels with a solid portion that connects the heels to the sole*
   Wedges seem to go in and out of style.

exercise   7-14

During the next week, look at the shoes of people on the street for examples of each type of shoe on the list, and make a note that describes each type and the person who is wearing it. Write your descriptions here.

1. sandals _____

2. boots _____

3. high heels _____

4. flats _____

5. wedges _____

6. pumps _____

7. Mary Janes _____

8. loafers _____

9. lace-ups _____

10. oxfords _____

11. sneakers _____

Words for Events

Parties

brunch: *a party where both breakfast and lunch dishes are served*
  Brunches are popular on Sunday mornings.

cocktail party: *a large party where drinks and snacks are served and where guests stand up and move around to talk to other guests*
  Cocktail parties are good places to meet new people.

dinner party: *a party where a formal evening meal is served*
  She has very elegant **dinner parties** and always invites interesting people.

engagement party: *a party to congratulate a couple on their commitment to marry one another*
  Her sister is having an **engagement party** for them.

get-together: *an informal party*
  Our group of friends has a **get-together** every month or so.

luncheon: *a party where a formal lunch is served*
  Her mother invited all of the wedding party to a **luncheon**.

open house: *a large party where the guests may arrive and leave at any time during the suggested hours*
  We were invited to an **open house** on New Year's Day.

party: *a group of people meeting together for the purpose of having fun*
I'm always ready for a **party**.

a group of people who do something together
The restaurant is reserving a table for a **party** of six people.

reception: *a party to meet, welcome, or say good-bye to someone*
The company invited me to a **reception** to meet the new vice president.

shower: *a party where the guests bring gifts for a bride-to-be or mother-to-be*
Our office is planning a **shower** for our assistant, who is expecting a baby in January.

wedding: *a ceremony to celebrate a marriage*
Were you invited to the **wedding**?

exercise | **7-15**

Write a few sentences telling what kind of party you like to attend and why you like that kind of party.

_____

_____

_____

_____

_____

Shows

comedy: *a play designed to make people laugh*
The play was a **comedy** about the humor in family life.

concert: *a music show*
The university students were excited about the **concert** given by their favorite band.

drama: *a serious play*
The play was a **drama** about serious issues in family life.

fashion show: *a show where models wear the latest fashions to introduce them to the public*
It's exciting to see the **fashion shows** in New York, Milan, and Paris.

game show: *a television show where people play games to win money or prizes*
She was on that **game show** and won a new car.

movie: *a motion picture or film*
What **movies** are playing in our neighborhood?

opera: *a play set to music*
We went to the **opera** when we were in Italy.

play: *a story written to be acted on a stage*
The high school seniors put on a **play** at the end of the year.

reality show: *a television show that films people as they live their own lives*
> A **reality show** can be funny or sad.

show: *an exhibition or entertainment for the public*
> The movie was an excellent **show**.

soap opera: *a TV show that shows daily episodes of a story that never ends*
> If you start watching a **soap opera**, it is hard to stop.

TV show: *a show broadcast on television*
> He doesn't want to stay home and watch **TV shows**.

exercise	7-16

Write a few sentences that name and describe a show you have seen recently.

_____

_____

_____

_____

_____

Games

board game: *a game played on a flat board specially designed for it, often with small pieces that belong to each player, and dice*
> **Board games** are fun for children and adults.

card game: *a game played with a standard deck of cards or cards specially designed for it; bridge, canasta, hearts, Old Maid, Go Fish, etc.*
> There are **card games** for children and for adults.

game: *an entertainment where two or more people compete with each other*
> Would you like to play a **game** with me?

hide-and-seek: *a children's game where one child, who is "it," must find another child in his or her hiding place, who then becomes "it"*
> **Hide-and-seek** is a game played everywhere.

match: *a tennis, soccer, or rugby game*
> I'd love to go to the movies, but I have a tennis **match** this afternoon.

parlor game: *an indoor game that is played among small groups of people at a party*
> Charades is a popular **parlor game**.

sports: *an athletic competition; a football game, a baseball game, a volleyball game, etc.*
> He loves to spend Sundays watching **sports**.

tag: *a children's game where one child, who is "it," must touch (tag) another, who then becomes "it"*
> **Tag** is a game played by children of all ages.

exercise   7-17

Match each type of game in the left column with one of the descriptions in the right column.

_____ 1. baseball game

a. four players sit around a table; one of them distributes a number of cards to all of the players; players try to win other players' cards, according to a set of rules

_____ 2. board game

b. two players stand on opposite sides of a net and hit a ball back and forth over the net with a racket; a score is made when a player cannot return the ball

_____ 3. card game

c. two teams of nine players each; players hit balls pitched to them by the other team, then try to run around three bases and then to home plate, where a score is made

_____ 4. children's game

d. three or four players arrange their pieces on a board and roll dice to see how many steps they can take in their goal of getting around the board first

_____ 5. parlor game

e. a number of children stand in a circle, while the child who is "it" drops a handkerchief behind one of them; that child then runs after the first one, tags him or her, and becomes "it"

_____ 6. tennis match

f. the guests at a party are divided into teams; one member of each team tries to help his or her teammates guess the answer to a problem, but with restrictions set by the rules of the game

Storms

cyclone: *a violent storm with rotating wind*
They changed their vacation plans because of the **cyclone** warning.

gale: *a wind with a speed between thirty-two and sixty-three miles per hour (between fifty and one hundred kilometers per hour)*
We'd better stay home. It looks like a **gale** outside.

hurricane: *a tropical storm with winds of seventy-four miles per hour (119 kilometers per hour) or greater*
The **hurricane** took the roof off our neighbor's house.

sandstorm: *a storm of sand in the desert*
During the **sandstorm** there were clouds of sand in the air.

storm: *a strong wind with rain, snow, or hail, and sometimes with thunder and lightning*
They had to stop driving because of the **storm**.

tornado: *a violent storm that whirls in a circular motion at speeds up to three hundred miles per hour*
Everyone must seek shelter; there is a **tornado** warning for the area.

exercise   7-18

Replace each italicized word with a more descriptive one.

1. There was a *storm* with winds of eighty miles an hour. _____

2. We stayed in from the *storm* because the winds were blowing at fifty miles an hour.

   _____

3. There was a violent *storm* in the desert. _____

4. The *storm* whirled around at 250 miles per hour, destroying everything.

   _____

PART II

ADJECTIVES

Adjectives are the words that allow us to be artists. Instead of painting the colors or making the music, we can use adjectives—*red, beautiful, lively, loud*—to describe the nouns in our lives.

Adjectives can be simple to use, as they don't change to fit the nouns they describe. For example, the same adjective can describe New York (a *big* city), New York and Los Angeles (*big* cities), or a noncount noun such as "furniture" (*big* furniture).

Adjectives can also be used to compare nouns with each other. To do this, certain adjectives have comparative and superlative forms that are made by adding *-er* or *-est* at the end, for example, "He is *taller* than his brother" or "He is the *tallest* boy in the class." Others are preceded by *more* or *most* to make these comparisons, for example, "She is *more patient* than the other teacher" or "She is the *most patient* teacher at the school."

When you know the patterns for using adjectives, it is easy to add new ones to your vocabulary. Enjoy adjectives and be creative!

Making Descriptions

Adjectives describe nouns and are usually placed before the nouns they describe:

> This is **good** food.

> He's a **nice** man.

> She has an **expensive** car.

> I got **cheap** tickets.

A form of the verb *be* can separate an adjective from the noun (or pronoun) it describes:

> The food is **good**.

> That man is **nice**.

> Her car is **expensive**.

> The tickets were **cheap**.

Two adjectives can be connected by the word *and*:

> Her car is **big** and **expensive**.

> The man is **smart** and **nice**.

A comma is used to separate adjectives when there are more than two:

> Her car is **big**, **comfortable**, and **expensive**.

> The man is **smart**, **nice**, and **handsome**.

Adjectives That Describe People

Adjectives describe a person's physical and personal characteristics. They answer the questions, "What are you like?" "What is she like?" "What is he like?" and "What are they like?" Review the words in the following list:

able	good	responsible
aggressive	handsome	rich
beautiful	interesting	silly
big	large	smart
brave	lazy	strict
charming	mean	sweet
fast	nice	tall
fat	old	unhappy
friendly	pretty	weak
funny	proud	
generous	quiet	

exercise   8-1

Fill in each blank with one or several words from the list.

1. I am _____ .

2. My neighbors are _____ .

3. A friend of mine is _____ .

4. I don't know anyone who is _____ .

5. Most of the people I see every day are _____ .

Antonyms

Antonyms are two words with opposite meanings. The adjectives in the following exercises are antonyms of the adjectives in the previous list, but not in the same order.

exercise   8-2

Fill in the antonym for each adjective using the list provided.

cowardly   handicapped   little   shy   slow   stingy   thin   ugly   unfriendly

1. able   _____

2. aggressive   _____

3. big   _____

4. brave   _____

5. beautiful   _____

6. fast   _____

7. fat _____

8. friendly _____

9. generous _____

exercise	8-3

Fill in the antonym for each adjective using the list provided.

bad   boring   energetic   humble   kind   noisy   plain   small   young

1. good _____

2. interesting _____

3. large _____

4. lazy _____

5. mean _____

6. old _____

7. pretty _____

8. proud _____

9. quiet _____

exercise	8-4

Fill in the antonym for each adjective using the list provided.

bitter   dumb   easygoing   happy   poor   serious   short   strong

1. rich _____

2. silly _____

3. smart _____

4. strict _____

5. sweet _____

6. tall _____

7. unhappy _____

8. weak _____

Prefixes

Many antonyms can be formed by adding a *prefix* to an adjective. The prefixes *in-*, *im-*, *ir-*, and *un-* all mean "not."

exercise   8-5

Fill in the antonym for each adjective using the prefixes indicated.

in-

EXAMPLE: active   *inactive*

1. capable   _____

2. competent   _____

3. considerate   _____

4. efficient   _____

5. secure   _____

6. sincere   _____

7. tolerant   _____

im-

EXAMPLE: mature   *immature*

8. modest   _____

9. patient   _____

10. polite   _____

11. proper   _____

ir-

EXAMPLE: responsible   *irresponsible*

12. resistible   _____

13. reverent   _____

un-

EXAMPLE: friendly   *unfriendly*

14. balanced   _____

15. civil   _____

16. civilized   _____

17. disciplined   _____

18. enthusiastic   _____

19. faithful   _____

20. fortunate   _____

21. happy   _____

22. healthy   _____

23. kind   _____

24. natural   _____

25. pleasant   _____

26. popular   _____

27. reasonable   _____

28. selfish   _____

29. successful   _____

30. tidy   _____

31. trustworthy   _____

32. truthful   _____

Suffixes

Some adjectives are formed by adding a *suffix* to a noun:

-ful

care	careful
cheer	cheerful
harm	harmful
skill	skillful
tact	tactful
success	successful
truth	truthful

Some (but not all) adjectives that end in *-ful* have antonyms that end in *-less*:

careful	**careless**
harmful	**harmless**
tactful	**tactless**

| exercise | 8-6 |

Write in the antonyms for the adjectives indicated. (Be careful—some of these are tricky!)

EXAMPLE: beautiful   *ugly*

1. careful   _____

2. faithful   _____

3. harmful   _____

4. successful   _____

5. tactful   _____

6. truthful   _____

The following are also adjective suffixes: *-ent, -able, -ible, -ic, -ly,* and *-ive.* Review the adjectives in the following chart:

-ent	-able	-ible	-ic	-ly	-ive
independent	adorable	flexible	athletic	cowardly	aggressive
insistent	hospitable	gullible	idealistic	friendly	appreciative
intelligent	likable	responsible	materialistic	lively	creative
persistent			optimistic	lonely	imaginative
			pessimistic	lovely	manipulative
					persuasive

| exercise | 8-7 |

Fill in each blank with the best word from the prefix group indicated.

-ent

1. A person who is smart is _____.

2. Someone who *persists* doesn't stop trying; that person is _____.

3. Someone who succeeds alone, who doesn't *depend* on help from others, is

_____.

4. People who demand action, or *insist* on it, are _____.

-able/-ible

5. People who welcome you to their home are _____.

6. A person who is pleasant, kind, helpful, and friendly is _____.

7. Someone who does his work well and on time is _____.

8. Babies are cute; when they smile they are _____.

9. A person who believes ridiculous stories is _____.

10. People who can adapt to others' needs are _____.

   -ic

11. People who expect a good future are _____.

12. People who expect a bad future are _____.

13. A person who is good at sports, such as tennis or football, is _____.

14. Someone who needs to own expensive things is _____.

15. A person who believes the future will be almost perfect is _____.

   -ly

16. A person who has a beautiful personality is _____.

17. Someone who has a lot of energy and enthusiasm is _____.

18. People who are afraid to act are _____.

19. A person who likes to talk to and help others is _____.

20. A person who has no friends is probably _____.

   -ive

21. *Creative* people have new ideas; they are _____.

22. A person who likes to control the actions of others is _____.

23. A person who gets other people to form an opinion is _____.

24. People who demand to be first are _____.

25. A person who is thankful is _____.

Using Adjectives with Other Words

A/ an, the, this, that, these, those, my, your, his, her, our, and *their* are *determiners.* An adjective goes between the determiner and the noun it describes:

> **the** irresponsible student
> **those** aggressive lawyers
> **my** adorable friend
> **our** athletic neighbor

The word *a* goes before an adjective that begins with a consonant sound; *an* goes before an adjective that begins with a vowel sound:

>**a** creative child
>**an** independent woman

exercise   8-8

Write a *or* an *in the blank before each adjective.*

1. He is _____ good friend.

2. She is _____ interesting girl.

3. My coworker is _____ optimistic person.

4. Her doctor is _____ capable surgeon.

5. That politician is _____ aggressive leader.

exercise   8-9

Use at least ten adjectives from this unit to describe yourself and other people you know. Be sure to write complete sentences.

1. _____

2. _____

3. _____

4. _____

5. _____

6. _____

7. _____

8. _____

9. _____

10. _____

Proper Adjectives

Proper adjectives describe people or things by their place of origin or group association. Proper adjectives are written with a capital letter:

African	European
African-American	Jewish
Asian	Mexican
Australian	Muslim
Buddhist	Native American
Canadian	North American
Caribbean	Japanese
Central American	South American
Christian	Western

exercise 8-10

Fill in the blanks with the appropriate proper adjectives.

1. Most of the people who live in my neighborhood are _____.

2. I work with a lot of _____ people.

3. I know only a few _____ people.

4. _____ music is my favorite.

5. _____ food is delicious.

Adjectives That Describe a Person's Condition

Adjectives describe a person's condition. They answer the questions, "How are you?" "How is she?" "How is he?" and "How are they?" Review the words in the following list:

busy	happy	so-so
calm	hungry	thirsty
cold	lost	tired
confused	nervous	upset
dead	ready	warm
dirty	satisfied	worried
fine	scared	
glad	sick	

exercise   **8-11**

Circle the word that best fills in each blank.

1. I had to eat something because I was so _____.

   worried   **hungry**   **thirsty**   **calm**

2. I didn't call you because I knew you were _____.

   busy   **so-so**   **dead**   **glad**

3. We are leaving at 6:00 tomorrow morning. Please be _____.

   worried   **scared**   **lost**   **ready**

4. If you are _____, get a drink from the refrigerator.

   satisfied   **confused**   **thirsty**   **dirty**

5. We're sorry you are _____ and hope you feel better soon.

   happy   **upset**   **glad**   **fine**

6. If you are too _____, put on a sweater.

   cold   **warm**   **tired**   **nervous**

Antonyms

Review the adjectives in the following list:

alive
anxious/upset/nervous
clean
cool
dissatisfied
full
hot
rested
sad/depressed
well

exercise   8-12

Find in the previous list the antonym for each of the following adjectives.

1. calm   _____

2. cold   _____

3. dead   _____

4. dirty   _____

5. happy   _____

6. hungry   _____

7. satisfied _____

8. sick   _____

9. tired   _____

10. warm   _____

The conjunction *but* between adjectives indicates contrast:

> I'm **fine** but **tired**.
> She is **sick** but **comfortable**.
> They are **hungry** but **happy**.
> We're **nervous** but **ready**.

exercise   8-13

Answer each question in complete sentences, using at least ten different adjectives. Connect two adjectives with and *or* but. *Use commas when you have more than two adjectives together.*

1. How are you today? _____

   _____

2. How is your best friend? _____

   _____

3. How is everyone in your family? _____

   _____

Adjectives That Describe Objects

Size

Review the following adjectives that describe things by their size:

little/small	medium-sized	big/large
tiny	average-sized	huge/enormous
narrow	of medium width	wide
short	of medium length	long
light	of medium weight	heavy

exercise 8-14

Write the antonyms for the following.

1. wide   _____

2. little   _____

3. heavy   _____

4. enormous   _____

5. long   _____

exercise 8-15

Describe by size five objects that you see right now. Be sure to write in complete sentences.

1. _____

2. _____

3. _____

4. _____

5. _____

Shape

Review the following adjectives that describe things by their shape:

diamond-shaped
rectangular
round
square
triangular

exercise	8-16

Answer each question in a complete sentence.

1. What do you see that is round?

   _____

2. What do you have that is square?

   _____

3. What traffic sign is triangular?

   _____

4. What is the shape of this book?

   _____

5. What is the shape of a baseball field?

   _____

Color

Review the following adjectives that describe things by their color:

black	green	pink	yellow
blue	gray	purple	white
brown	orange	red	

A color mixed with white is called "light": light blue, light green. A color mixed with black is called "dark": dark red, dark purple. Fashion colors are often named after flowers, fruit, or other natural items: rose, lilac, turquoise, tomato, avocado, chocolate, bark.

exercise	8-17

Describe five things you see by their color. Use complete sentences.

1. _____

2. _____

3. _____

4. _____

5. _____

Quality

Review the following adjectives that describe things by their quality:

acceptable	inefficient
cheap	inferior
comfortable	shoddy
convenient	special
cozy	sturdy
delicious	superior
effective	terrible
efficient	unacceptable
excellent	uncomfortable
expensive	unimportant
favorite	useful
inconvenient	useless
inedible	well-made
ineffective	wobbly

exercise   8-18

Match the adjectives in the left column with their antonyms in the right column.

_____ 1. acceptable   a. expensive

_____ 2. cheap   b. inconvenient

_____ 3. comfortable   c. inedible

_____ 4. convenient   d. ineffective

_____ 5. delicious   e. inferior

_____ 6. effective   f. shoddy

_____ 7. excellent   g. terrible

_____ 8. special   h. unacceptable

_____ 9. sturdy   i. uncomfortable

_____ 10. superior   j. unimportant

_____ 11. useful   k. useless

_____ 12. well-made   l. wobbly

Condition

Review the following adjectives that describe things by their condition:

broken	neat
clean	new
dirty	old
dusty	patched
empty	ragged
fixed	ruined
fresh	spoiled/rotten
full	tidy
like-new	torn
messy	worn

exercise | 8-19

Write the antonym to each of the following adjectives.

1. full _____

2. old _____

3. torn _____

4. neat _____

5. clean _____

6. fixed _____

7. rotten _____

exercise | 8-20

Describe the condition of five things you have.

1. _____

2. _____

3. _____

4. _____

5. _____

Adjectives That Describe Places

Review the following adjectives that describe places:

airy	light
badly designed	modern
badly located	old-fashioned
cheap	open
cramped	private
crowded	rundown
damp	safe
dangerous	spacious
dark	unfurnished
dry	well-built
empty	well-designed
expensive	well-located
furnished	well-maintained

exercise   8-21

Find the antonyms to the following adjectives in the previous list, and write them in the blanks:

1. cheap   _____

2. cramped   _____

3. crowded   _____

4. damp   _____

5. dangerous   _____

6. dark   _____

7. furnished   _____

8. rundown   _____

9. private   _____

10. modern   _____

exercise	8-22

Use at least ten adjectives from the previous list to describe the place you are in right now.

1. _____

2. _____

3. _____

4. _____

5. _____

6. _____

7. _____

8. _____

9. _____

10. _____

Adjectives That Describe the Weather

Review the adjectives in the following list:

breezy	humid
chilly	icy
clear	nice
cloudy	pleasant
cold	rainy
cool	stormy
dry	sunny
foggy	unpleasant
freezing	warm
hot	windy

| exercise | 8-23 |

Complete the following chart by listing the adjectives that describe pleasant weather and those that describe unpleasant weather.

Pleasant Weather	Unpleasant Weather
_____	_____
_____	_____
_____	_____
_____	_____
_____	_____
_____	_____
_____	_____
_____	_____
_____	_____

| exercise | 8-24 |

Fill in the blanks with the most appropriate words from the previous list.

1. I don't like to go out on a(n) _____ day.

2. In January the weather is often _____.

3. In May it is usually _____ where I live.

4. Today where I live it is _____.

5. People often go swimming when it is _____.

6. It is dangerous to drive when it is _____.

7. It's good to have an umbrella on a _____ day.

8. It's a good idea to wear a hat when it is _____.

9. A hat can blow off if it is _____.

10. You need a light jacket when it is _____.

Comparisons and Superlatives

Making an Adjective Stronger or Weaker

Review the following chart:

not at all < not very < a little < somewhat < rather < pretty < very < extremely

not at all = The adjective mentioned does not describe the noun.

The tickets are **not at all** cheap.

not very = The noun does not have much of the quality of the adjective.

That area is **not very** safe.

a little = The noun has only a little bit of the quality of the adjective.

The car is **a little** expensive.

somewhat = The noun has some of the quality of the adjective.

The food is **somewhat** spicy.

rather = The noun has quite a few aspects of the quality of the adjective.

It's a **rather** large class.

pretty = The noun has a lot of the quality of the adjective.

It's a **pretty** long trip.

very = The noun is a good example of the quality of the adjective.

They're **very** good books.

extremely   =   The noun is a superior example of the quality of the adjective.

It's an **extremely** hard course.

Fill in the blanks with the word from the previous list that best completes each sentence.

1. My sister's job is to feed the neighbor's cats. Her job is _____ easy.

2. My friend bought a car for $100. His car was _____ expensive.

3. Our neighbor has a dog that barks all night. Our neighbor's dog is

   _____ noisy.

4. Their house is near the metro station and the bus stop. Their house is in a

   _____ convenient location.

5. She invited about fifty people to her house for a celebration. She had a

   _____ large party.

exercise   9-2

Now complete the following sentences with the same types of expressions.

1. My job is _____ easy.

2. My shoes were _____ expensive.

3. My neighbor's dog is _____ friendly.

4. My house is in a _____ convenient location.

5. My dinner last night was _____ salty.

Expressing Negative Effects

The word *too* before an adjective indicates that the adjective is so strong that it has a negative effect:

That car is **too expensive**. (I can't buy it.)
He is **too rich**. (He values money over people.)
They were **too tired**. (They couldn't work.)
The party was **too noisy**. (The police came and sent everybody home.)

exercise	9-3

After each sentence with too, *write a possible negative effect.*

1. The food was too cold. _____

2. It was too rainy. _____

3. I ate too much cake. _____

4. She was driving too fast. _____

5. The shoes are too small. _____

exercise	9-4

Write five sentences that describe yourself or people you know. Use five of these expressions: not at all, a little, somewhat, rather, pretty, very, extremely, too.

1. _____

2. _____

3. _____

4. _____

5. _____

Making Comparisons with Adjectives

Nouns are compared with other nouns by the strength of their adjectives. An adjective made stronger is followed by the word *than* in a comparison.

One-Syllable Adjectives

Adjectives that have only one syllable are made stronger by adding the suffix *-er*:

She is **taller than** her sister.
He is **faster than** the other runner.
These tickets were **cheaper than** those.
It is **colder** in the north **than** in the south.

exercise   9-5

Write the stronger form of each of the following adjectives.

1. bright   _____

2. cheap   _____

3. clean   _____

4. cold   _____

5. cool   _____

6. damp   _____

7. dark   _____

8. fast   _____

9. fresh   _____

10. high   _____

11. light   _____

12. long   _____

13. neat   _____

14. new   _____

15. old   _____

16. plain   _____

17. poor   _____

18. rich   _____

19. short   _____

20. sick   _____

21. slow   _____

22. small   _____

23. smart   _____

24. sweet   _____

25. tall   _____

26. young   _____

Adjectives that have one syllable and that end in *-e* are made stronger by adding *-r*:

He is **nicer than** his brother.
They are **cuter than** they were before.

exercise   9-6

Write the stronger form of each of the following adjectives.

1. cute   _____

2. fine   _____

3. lame   _____

4. loose   _____

5. nice   _____

6. pale   _____

7. rude   _____

8. tame   _____

9. wide   _____

A few one-syllable adjectives end in *-w, -x,* or *-y*. These are made stronger by adding *-er*:

low	**lower**
new	**newer**
slow	**slower**
lax	**laxer**
gray	**grayer**

Other adjectives of one syllable that end in a consonant-vowel-consonant are made stronger by repeating the final consonant and adding *-er*:

She is **bigger** than he is.
I think she's **thinner** than she was before.

exercise   9-7

Write the stronger form of each of the following adjectives.

1. big   _____

2. fat   _____

3. fit   _____

4. hot   _____

5. mad   _____

6. red   _____

7. sad   _____

8. thin   _____

The comparative (stronger) forms of *good* and *bad* are irregular:

That was a **good** movie, but this one is **better**.
She had **bad** luck, and now it is **worse**.

exercise   9-8

Use good, bad, better, *or* worse *to complete the sentences.*

1. Today's weather is _____. Yesterday's was _____.

2. The job I have is _____. It is _____ than the one I had before.

3. The condition of my room is _____. It is _____ than it was last week.

4. Today I feel _____. I feel _____ than I did yesterday.

Two-Syllable Adjectives

A lot of adjectives have two syllables and end in *-y*. They are made stronger by changing the *y* to *i* and adding *-er*:

He is **happier** now.
I hope it will be **sunnier** tomorrow.
That movie is **funnier** than the last one we saw.

exercise	9-9

Write the stronger form of each of the following adjectives.

1. angry   _____

2. bossy   _____

3. busy   _____

4. cloudy   _____

5. cozy   _____

6. crazy   _____

7. dirty   _____

8. easy   _____

9. friendly   _____

10. funny   _____

11. happy   _____

12. lazy   _____

13. lonely   _____

14. lovely   _____

15. lucky   _____

16. noisy   _____

17. pretty   _____

18. rainy   _____

19. silly   _____

20. sunny   _____

21. tasty   _____

22. ugly   _____

A few adjectives that have two syllables are made stronger by adding *-r* (if they end in *-e*) or *-er*:

cruel	**crueler**
gentle	**gentler**
little	**littler**
narrow	**narrower**
quiet	**quieter**
simple	**simpler**

This street is **narrower** than that one.
This exercise is **simpler** than the other one.

exercise   9-10

Fill in each blank with the comparative form of the best adjective from the previous list.

1. It was noisy last night, but now it is _____.

2. The last problem was complicated. This one is _____.

3. The streets in that town are _____ than the avenues in the city.

4. At first he was too rough with the puppy, but now he is _____.

5. The first king was cruel, and this one is _____.

6. This little girl has a baby sister who is _____ than she is.

Most adjectives that have two or more syllables are made stronger by placing the word *more* before them:

more modern	**more** wonderful	**more** responsible
more famous	**more** dangerous	**more** imaginative

exercise   9-11

Write the comparative form of each adjective. Some will end in -er; others will have more *before them.*

1. athletic _____

2. boring _____

3. civil _____

4. civilized _____

5. clean _____

6. comfortable _____

7. considerate _____

8. cool _____

9. delicious _____

10. dirty _____

11. fresh _____

12. friendly _____

13. gentle _____

14. gullible _____

15. healthy _____

16. hot _____

17. open _____

18. patient _____

19. persuasive _____

20. pleasant _____

21. proper _____

22. proud _____

23. quiet _____

24. rude _____

25. sad _____

26. serious _____

27. sick _____

28. silly _____

29. sincere _____

30. slow _____

31. small _____

32. stingy _____

33. successful   _____

34. sweet   _____

35. tiny   _____

36. unfriendly   _____

37. upset   _____

38. useful   _____

39. wide   _____

40. worried   _____

Making Adjectives Weaker

All adjectives can be made weaker by placing the words *not as* before them:

> This apple is **not as** good as the other one.
> Those dresses are **not as** pretty as these.
> These shoes are **not as** comfortable as my old ones.

In a comparison a stronger adjective is followed by *than*; a weaker adjective is followed by *as*:

> This desk is **sturdier than** that one.
> That chair is **not as comfortable as** this one.

exercise   9-12

In each blank, make the adjective in parentheses stronger or weaker, as appropriate.

1. I bought this dress because it was (pretty) _____ the others in the shop.

2. He took the shoes back to the store because they were (comfortable)

   _____ his old ones.

3. I didn't go back to that restaurant because the food was (good)

   _____ I had expected.

4. We stayed a long time at the party, because it was (good) _____ the last one.

5. The new car is nice, but it's (big) _____ the old one.

Expressing Superlatives

Superlative adjectives indicate that a noun has more of the adjective's quality than two or more other nouns:

John is five feet ten inches tall.	James is six feet tall.	Bill is six feet two inches tall.
John is tall.	James is taller than John.	Bill is taller than John and James.
		Bill is the **tallest** in the class.

Adjectives that end in -er in the comparative form end in -est in the superlative form:

bigger	**biggest**
cooler	**coolest**
nicer	**nicest**
quieter	**quietest**
sillier	**silliest**
simpler	**simplest**

The superlative forms of *good* and *bad* are irregular:

good	**best**
bad	**worst**

exercise   9-13

Write the superlative form of each adjective.

1. bad _____

2. clean _____

3. cold _____

4. crazy _____

5. cute _____

6. friendly _____

7. gentle _____

8. good _____

9. hot _____

10. silly _____

11. lucky _____

12. mad _____

13. neat   _____

14. nice   _____

15. rude   _____

16. sad   _____

exercise   9-14

Choose five of the superlatives in the answers to Exercise 9-13 to describe five people you know.

1. _____

2. _____

3. _____

4. _____

5. _____

Adjectives that are preceded by *more* in their comparative form are preceded by *most* in their superlative form:

more appreciative   **most appreciative**
more difficult   **most difficult**
more modern   **most modern**
more responsible   **most responsible**

exercise   9-15

Write the superlative form of each adjective.

1. active   _____

2. bad   _____

3. cold   _____

4. comfortable   _____

5. fast   _____

6. flexible   _____

7. generous   _____

8. happy _____

9. large _____

10. little _____

11. new _____

12. noisy _____

13. serious _____

14. ugly _____

15. uninteresting _____

16. useless _____

exercise 9-16

Choose five of the superlatives in the answers to Exercise 9-15 to describe five people you know or things you have.

1. _____

2. _____

3. _____

4. _____

5. _____

Verbs and Nouns Used as Adjectives

Verbs Used as Adjectives

The *present participle* and the *past participle* of some verbs can be used as adjectives. The *present participle* is the form that ends in *-ing* (see also page 42):

surprise	It is **surprising** news.
excite	You have an **exciting** job.
bore	That is a **boring** program.

Review the present participles in the following list:

boring	gratifying
captivating	inspiring
caring	interesting
confusing	satisfying
daring	surprising
exciting	terrifying
fascinating	threatening
frustrating	

These adjectives describe a person or thing that "performs the action of the verb."

A **caring** mother	=	a mother who *cares for* her children.
A **boring** movie	=	a movie that *bores* the audience.
A **threatening** storm	=	a storm that *threatens* to begin soon.

exercise 10-1

Select the word that best completes each sentence:

1. We left the movie before it ended because it was _____.

   caring   captivating   boring   exciting

2. The math test was too hard for me; I thought the word problems were very

   _____.

   frustrating   exciting   boring   satisfying

3. I don't like horror movies because they are _____.

   interesting   terrifying   inspiring   gratifying

4. Helping other people is extremely _____.

   threatening   confusing   gratifying   terrifying

5. That novel has a lot of different stories happening at the same time; it is very

   _____.

   caring   terrifying   surprising   confusing

6. The circus trapeze artist performed a lot of dangerous stunts. He was a

   _____ young man.

   daring   confusing   frustrating   threatening

The *past participle* of the verb can also be used as an adjective. This is the verb form that often ends in *-ed* or *-en*. There are also quite a few irregular past participles that have different endings. (See page 144.) Following are examples of past participles that are commonly used as adjectives:

She is **excited** about her trip.
The toy is **broken**.
We were **surprised** to hear the news.
The child is **lost**.

Review the past participles in the following list:

broken	gratified	surprised
captivated	grown	terrified
closed	hidden	threatened
confused	inspired	torn
dead	interested	upset
drunk	lost	withdrawn
excited	married	worn
fascinated	satisfied	wounded
forbidden	shut	woven
forgotten	sold	written
found	spoken	
frustrated	stolen	

exercise   10-2

Choose appropriate words from the previous list to fill in the blanks.

1. She needed glasses to read the _____ words.

2. He couldn't hear the _____ words.

3. Police detectives are searching for the _____ painting.

4. It is very dangerous to drive if you are _____.

5. She lives alone now, as her children are all _____.

6. The _____ soldiers were taken to a hospital.

7. _____ fabric is sturdier than knitted fabric.

8. He used his _____ T-shirt for a rag.

9. The people could not read that book because it was on the king's list of

   _____ books.

10. Our new neighbor doesn't talk very much; she is shy and _____.

Often, the *present participle* adjective defines the *cause* of something. The *past participle* adjective defines the *person affected*:

The information was **surprising**.	We were **surprised**.
The game was **exciting**.	The fans were **excited**.
The girl is **fascinating**.	The man is **fascinated**.

exercise	10-3

Select the present participle *adjective or the* past participle *adjective, depending on which best completes each sentence.*

1. We thought the movie was **fascinating/fascinated**.

2. The children were not very **interesting/interested** in the story.

3. That is very **surprising/surprised** news.

4. I thought the questions were **confusing/confused**.

5. That movie was so scary, I was really **terrifying/terrified**.

6. When the band arrived, we were very **exciting/excited**.

7. My friend was **captivating/captivated** by that novel.

8. That store has a lot of **satisfying/satisfied** customers.

9. Waiting in line can be very **frustrating/frustrated**.

10. We were **inspiring/inspired** by our leader's speech.

Nouns Used as Adjectives

Certain nouns can be used as adjectives to tell what the noun described is made of:

a **cardboard** box   =   a box made of cardboard
a **glass** table   =   a table made of glass

exercise	10-4

Write definitions for the following items.

1. a gold necklace _____

2. a metal hook _____

3. a plastic tray _____

4. a silver bracelet _____

5. an oak floor _____

6. a wicker basket _____

7. a dirt road _____

8. a silk blouse _____

9. a wool skirt _____

10. a cotton blanket _____

Certain nouns can be used as adjectives to tell what the noun described is meant to contain. In some cases the two words are written together as one word:

| a **mailbox** | = | a box for mail |
| a **bookcase** | = | a case for books |

exercise   10-5

Write definitions for the following items.

1. a jewelry box _____

2. an ashtray _____

3. a trash can _____

4. a picture frame _____

5. a flour sack _____

6. a key ring _____

7. a grocery bag _____

8. a glove compartment _____

9. a lunchbox _____

10. a garbage pail _____

Certain nouns can be used as adjectives to tell the purpose of the noun described:

A **potato** peeler is used for peeling potatoes.
A **dishwasher** is used for washing dishes.

exercise | **10-6**

Write what each of the following is used for.

1. a nutcracker _____

2. a can opener _____

3. a fire extinguisher _____

4. a CD player _____

5. an ice pick _____

6. a hair dryer _____

7. nail polish remover _____

8. a pencil sharpener _____

9. spot remover _____

10. a floor polisher _____

Certain nouns can be used as adjectives to tell what is sold in the type of store described:

| a **shoe** store | = | a store where shoes are sold |
| a **grocery** store | = | a store where groceries are sold |

exercise | **10-7**

Write five other types of stores or shops.

1. _____

2. _____

3. _____

4. _____

5. _____

Certain nouns define other nouns by their type:

| a **motorcycle** | = | a cycle with a motor |
| **schoolwork** | = | work that is done at school |

exercise   10-8

Write the names of the items described.

1. a lock for a bicycle   _____

2. a key for a mailbox   _____

3. a garden of roses   _____

4. work that is done at home   _____

5. a desk for a student   _____

Some adjectives are formed by adding the suffix *-ed* to a noun. These adjectives often follow another descriptive adjective to which it is closed up or connected by a hyphen:

a three-**legged** stool	=	a stool with three legs
a red**headed** woodpecker	=	a woodpecker (bird) with a red head
a brown-**eyed** girl	=	a girl with brown eyes

Review the following noun + *-ed* adjectives:

evenhanded	fair, just
hardheaded	stubborn
hard-nosed	hardheaded
hotheaded	temperamental
levelheaded	sensible
long-winded	capable of giving long, boring speeches
single-minded	focused on one goal
sure-footed	cautious, secure

exercise   10-9

Circle the most appropriate adjective to fill in each blank.

1. We didn't want to do business with him because he was so _____.

   evenhanded   **hardheaded**   **sure-footed**

2. I wasn't worried on the hike because our leader was _____.

   hard-nosed   **sure-footed**   **long-winded**

3. He got the job done efficiently because of his _____ approach.

   single-minded   **long-winded**   **hotheaded**

4. The meeting went on for hours because of too many _____ speakers.

    sure-footed   **single-minded**   **long-winded**

5. The school principal treats all cases equally; she is very _____.

    evenhanded   **single-minded**   **hard-nosed**

6. Try not to make him angry. He's so _____ he might make a scene.

    single-minded   **sure-footed**   **hotheaded**

Compound Adjectives

A noun connected to its modifiers by hyphens can be used as an adjective. The noun is used in singular form, even though it is modified by a plural marker:

a **twenty-dollar** ticket	=	a ticket that costs twenty dollars
a **ten-foot** pole	=	a pole that is ten feet long
a **two-year** lease	=	a lease that lasts two years

exercise   **10-10**

Write definitions for the following.

1. a five-year plan _____

2. a three-year warranty _____

3. a lifetime guarantee _____

4. a ten-minute discussion _____

5. a three-pound weight _____

6. a two-week vacation _____

7. a two-year contract _____

8. an all-day meeting _____

9. an all-night party _____

10. an everyday occurrence _____

Adjective Order

When two or three adjectives are used together, they are usually in the following order:

1. quality
2. condition
3. size
4. age
5. shape
6. color
7. origin
8. material
9. type

a **beautiful old** house	(quality, age)
a **nice clean white** uniform	(quality, condition, color)
a **shiny new red** bicycle	(condition, age, color)

exercise 11-1

Rewrite the adjectives in the correct order to describe the indicated nouns.

1. skirt: silk, long, black _____

2. shoes: leather, Italian, new _____

3. earrings: silver, beautiful, Mexican _____

4. cake: birthday, rich, three-layer _____

5. mirror: heavy, antique, round _____

exercise   11-2

Describe five of your favorite things, using two or three descriptive adjectives for each one.

1. _____

2. _____

3. _____

4. _____

5. _____

PART III

VERBS

Verbs are the wonderful words that give life to language.

The most common verb, *be*, for example, allows us to tell who or what exists in the world, and also when, where, how, and why it exists. In addition, just by changing the form of the verb, we can tell about what existed in the past and what will exist in the future, plus what we wish existed or what we would do if something existed. The verb *be* is used in a different manner from all other English verbs—it has different forms and different patterns.

All other verbs follow a second set of patterns, which enable us to tell facts about people—where and how they live, what they have, how they look and feel, what they like, what they think, and what they do; they also enable us to tell how things work and what happens in the world. And again, with a change in form, we can put all this information in the past or the future, or we can make wishes and conjectures.

Verbs also enable us to ask and answer questions, give commands and suggestions, accept or refuse, and relate and communicate.

Yes, there are a lot of irregular forms that have to be memorized, but they are worth the effort. Verbs are about life. Live well with verbs!

The Verb *Be*

The most common verb is *be*. It is used to identify or describe a person or thing, or to tell its origin, state, or location.

The Present Tense of *Be*

I **am** tall.
You **are** my friend.
He **is** sick.
She **is** a smart girl.
It **is** a mistake.

We **are** at home.
You (all) **are** great helpers.
They **are** from South America.

exercise 12-1

Fill in each blank with the appropriate form of be *in the present tense.*

1. Bill _____ here.

2. Janet and Mary Jane _____ good friends.

3. Emily _____ on vacation.

4. Betty and I _____ teachers.

5. You _____ a good student.

6. I _____ not tired.

exercise	12-2

Answer each of the following questions in a complete sentence using the verb be.

1. What is your name? _____

2. Where are you from? _____

3. Who are your best friends? _____

4. Where are your best friends now? _____

5. What is in your hand? _____

6. What color is it? _____

Asking Questions with *Be*

Questions with the verb *be* are formed by reversing the subject and the verb:

I am	**Am I . . . ?**	We are	**Are we . . . ?**
You are	**Are you . . . ?**	They are	**Are they . . . ?**
He is	**Is he . . . ?**		
She is	**Is she . . . ?**		
It is	**Is it . . . ?**		

exercise	12-3

Change the following statements to questions.

1. He is here now. _____

2. You are happy. _____

3. I am sitting down. _____

4. He is asking directions. _____

5. They are building a new house. _____

6. She is turning left. _____

7. He is taking photographs. _____

8. She is riding a bicycle. _____

Making *Be* Negative

Sentences with *be* are made negative by placing **not** after the conjugated form:

I am **not** tired.   We are **not** working.
You are **not** smiling.   You all are **not** running.
He is **not** sitting in the park.   They are **not** sitting in the park.
She is **not** at home.
It is **not** earning interest.

Negatives are usually contracted:

I'm not   We **aren't**
You **aren't**   You (all) **aren't**
He **isn't**   They **aren't**
She **isn't**
It **isn't**

exercise   12-4

Make each of the sentences in Exercise 12-3 negative.

1. _____

2. _____

3. _____

4. _____

5. _____

6. _____

7. _____

8. _____

The Past Tense of *Be*

I **was** in the city.   We **were** very happy.
You **were** shy.   You (all) **were** at school.
He **was** sick.   They **were** broken.
She **was** not tired.
It **was** good.

exercise   12-5

Change the answers in Exercise 12-1 to the past tense.

1. _____

2. _____

3. _____

4. _____

5. _____

6. _____

exercise   12-6

Answer each question in a complete sentence using the past tense of be.

1. Where were you yesterday at 4:00? _____

2. Who was with you? _____

3. Were you indoors or outdoors? _____

4. How was the weather? _____

5. Were there other people there? _____

Unit 13

Non—*To Be* Verbs

Review the words in the following list that have meanings similar to *be*:

appear
become
feel
look
look like
resemble
seem
smell
sound

Regular Present Tense Forms of Verbs Other than *Be*

The basic verb is used with *I, you, we,* and *they*:

I **look** tired.   We **look** silly.

You **look** sick.   They **look** beautiful.

The basic verb + the suffix *-s* is used with *he, she,* and *it*:

He **looks** good.

She **looks** better.

It **looks** dirty.

| **exercise** | **13-1** |

Match the sentences in the left column with those in the right column.

_____ 1. She is blonde and her mother is blonde.   a. He appears angry.

_____ 2. They are smiling.   b. He looks like me.

_____ 3. You should throw it in the garbage.   c. I feel sick.

_____ 4. We need to rest.   d. It becomes boring.

_____ 5. I like the music.   e. It smells bad.

_____ 6. She is crying.   f. It sounds good.

_____ 7. His face is red.   g. She feels sad.

_____ 8. I have brown eyes. He has brown eyes.   h. She resembles her mother.

_____ 9. It is a long book.   i. They seem happy.

_____10. I need to lie down.   j. We look tired.

| **exercise** | **13-2** |

Choose the word that best completes each sentence.

1. The music **becomes/sounds** great.

2. The girls **resemble/appear** tired.

3. We **feel/smell** tired.

4. The flowers **become/smell** wonderful.

5. He **seems/resembles** angry.

6. She **seems/resembles** her mother.

Spelling Changes in *He/She/It* Forms

The verbs *go* and *do* add *-es*:

He **goes**.
She **does**.

Verbs that end in *-ch* or *-sh* add *-es*:

He **watches**.
She **washes**.

Verbs that end in -*y* change the *y* to *i* and add -*es*:

> He **cries**.
> She **tries**.

The *he/she/it* form of the verb *have* is *has*:

> He **has** a cold.
> She **has** the flu.

exercise	13-3

Write the present tense he/she/it *forms of the following verbs.*

1. match   _____

2. eat   _____

3. have   _____

4. drink   _____

5. go   _____

6. wish   _____

7. clean   _____

8. dry   _____

9. do   _____

10. dance   _____

Regular Past Tense Forms

The past tense of most verbs is formed by adding the suffix -*ed* to the basic verb:

appear	**appeared**
look	**looked**
seem	**seemed**
sound	**sounded**

The same form is used for *I, you, he, she, it, we,* and *they*:

> They **appeared** tired.
> She **looked** pretty.
> He **seemed** nice.
> It **sounded** good.

exercise   13-4

Write the past tense forms of the following verbs.

1. clean   _____

2. open   _____

3. work   _____

4. walk   _____

5. watch   _____

Spelling Changes in Past Tense Forms

Verbs that end in -*e* add -*d*:

change   **changed**
resemble   **resembled**

One-syllable verbs that end in a vowel + a consonant repeat the consonant and add -*ed*. (Many verbs that end in a vowel + a consonant are irregular. See page 119.)

beg   **begged**
hop   **hopped**

Verbs that end in -*y* change the *y* to *i* and add -*ed*:

cry   **cried**
study   **studied**

exercise   13-5

Write the past tense forms of the following verbs.

1. stop   _____

2. close   _____

3. shop   _____

4. exercise   _____

5. try   _____

Verbs That Describe Usual Activities

Review the verbs in the following list:

brush (your teeth)	plan
call (your friends)	play
clean	rest
close (the door)	smile
comb (your hair)	talk
cook	turn (off the light)
cry	turn (on the light)
dream	walk
exercise	wash (your hands)
laugh	watch
listen	work
open (the door)	

exercise   13-6

Write the past tense form of each of the following verbs.

1. listen   _____

2. laugh   _____

3. turn   _____

4. dream   _____

5. cry   _____

6. exercise   _____

7. brush   _____

8. smile   _____

9. plan   _____

10. watch   _____

Telling How Often an Activity Is Performed

never < rarely/seldom < sometimes < often < a lot < every day < always

I **never** watch TV.	We **often** play together.
She **rarely** calls her friends.	You (all) laugh **a lot**.
Sometimes he rests in the afternoon.	They work **every day**.
	They **always** smile.

exercise	13-7

Choose ten activities from the previous list, and write a sentence for each that tells how often you do each activity. Use the present tense.

1. _____

2. _____

3. _____

4. _____

5. _____

6. _____

7. _____

8. _____

9. _____

10. _____

More Daily Activities

Review the verbs in the following list:

come (home)   make (the bed)
drink (water)   put (on your clothes)
drive   read
eat   ride
eat/have (breakfast)   sit (down)
eat/have (dinner)   sleep
eat/have (lunch)   stand (up)
get (dressed)   take (a bath)
get (up)   take (a shower)
go (to a place)   take (off your clothes)
go (to bed)   think
lie (down)   wake (up)

exercise	13-8

Choose ten verbs from the previous list and tell how often you perform each activity. Use complete sentences.

1. _____

2. _____

3. _____

4. _____

5. _____

6. _____

7. _____

8. _____

9. _____

10. _____

Irregular Past Tense Forms

All of the verbs in the previous list have irregular past tense forms. The past tense form is listed after the slash (/):

come/came
drink/drank
drive/drove
eat/ate
get/got
go/went
lie/lay
make/made
put/put
read/read
ride/rode
sit/sat
sleep/slept
stand/stood
take/took
think/thought
wake/woke

exercise   13-9

Using verbs from the previous list in the past tense, write ten sentences that tell what you did yesterday.

1. _____

2. _____

3. _____

4. _____

5. _____

6. _____

7. _____

8. _____

9. _____

10. _____

Verbs Used for Household Activities

Review the verbs in the following list. If the past tense form is irregular, it is indicated following the slash (/):

clean (the house)
clean (up the mess)
clean (up the yard)
do (laundry)/did
do (the shopping)/did
dust (the furniture)
empty (the dishwasher)
iron (clothes)
load (the dishwasher)
make (appointments)/made
make (repairs)/made

mow (the lawn)
pay (bills)/paid
put (the groceries away)/put
scrub (floors)
sweep (the floor)/swept
take (out the trash)/took
vacuum
wash (the windows)
water (plants)
weed (the garden)

exercise   13-10

Fill in the blanks using the present tense of the verbs in parentheses.

1. John (make) _____ repairs.

2. I (water) _____ the plants.

3. My friends (clean) _____ the house.

4. Mary and Jack (vacuum) _____.

5. My dad (pay) _____ the bills.

Telling When an Activity Is Performed

in the morning
in the afternoon
in the evening
in the fall
in the spring
in the summer
in the winter

at night
at 1:00
at 2:15
at 3:30
at 4:45
at 5:55
at 7:10

on Mondays
on Tuesdays
on Wednesdays
on Thursdays
on Fridays
on Saturdays
on Sundays

on holidays
on my birthday
on the first day of the month
on the tenth of June
on weekends

in January
in February
in March
in April
in May
in June
in July
in August
in September
in October
in November
in December

every day
every month
every night
every week

| **exercise** | **13-11** |

Complete each sentence by telling when the person indicated does the activity in parentheses.

1. I (rest) _____.

2. My best friend (exercise) _____.

3. My neighbors (walk) _____.

4. My friends and I (eat together) _____.

5. I (call my friends) _____.

| **exercise** | **13-12** |

Complete each sentence by telling which activities you usually perform at the times indicated.

1. On Mondays _____.

2. In the summer _____.

3. On weekends _____.

4. In the morning _____.

5. Every day _____.

| **exercise** | **13-13** |

Fill in each blank with the most appropriate verb from the list of household activities.

1. She uses a broom to _____.

2. I take the car to _____.

3. I use the iron to _____.

4. He uses the telephone to _____.

5. We use a wet rag to _____.

6. He takes out his checkbook to _____.

7. He uses a screwdriver to _____.

8. They go outside to _____.

9. We need a washer and dryer to _____.

10. I use a dry cloth to _____.

exercise | 13-14

Write five sentences that tell which of the activities on the household activities list you usually did when you were a child. Write the verbs in the past tense.

1. _____
2. _____
3. _____
4. _____
5. _____

Verbs Used in a Classroom

Review the verbs in the following list. Irregular past tense forms are indicated after the slash (/):

answer	play
ask (questions)	read/read
correct (mistakes)	solve (a problem)
do (exercises)/did	spell
draw (a picture)/drew	study
erase	take (a test)/took
help (someone)	take (turns)/took
learn	teach/taught
listen (to someone)	understand/understood
make (a mistake)/made	use (the computer)
pay (attention)/paid	write/wrote

exercise | 13-15

Write the past tense forms of the following verbs.

1. answer _____
2. ask _____
3. correct _____
4. erase _____
5. help _____

6. learn   _____

7. listen   _____

8. pay   _____

9. play   _____

10. solve   _____

11. spell   _____

12. study   _____

13. use   _____

exercise   13-16

Fill in each blank with the past tense of the verb indicated.

1. My mother (teach) _____ me to read and write.

2. He (write) _____ her an e-mail last week.

3. I (understand) _____ today's lesson.

4. We (take) _____ a hard test this morning.

5. You (make) _____ only one mistake.

6. They (do) _____ all of the exercises.

7. They (draw) _____ pictures in class.

8. My friend and I (take) _____ turns with the computer.

9. She (read) _____ us a wonderful story.

10. I hope you (pay) _____ attention.

Making Verbs Negative

In the present tense, all verbs except *be* are made negative by placing *do not* or *does not* before them.

Do not is used for *I, you, we,* and *they.* It is often contracted to *don't.*

Does not is used with *he, she,* and *it.* It is often contracted to *doesn't.*

I **don't** weed the garden.
You **don't** rest.
He **doesn't** exercise.
She **doesn't** smile.

We **don't** sleep late.
You (all) **don't** wake up early.
They **don't** clean up the yard.

exercise 13-17

Rewrite the following sentences, making them negative and using the contracted form.

1. He gets up at 6:00.

   _____

2. They eat breakfast together every morning.

   _____

3. She dreams during the day.

   _____

4. We buy groceries every week.

   _____

5. I laugh a lot.

   _____

In the past tense, verbs are made negative by placing *did not* before them.

Did not is often contracted to *didn't*:

I **didn't** comb my hair.
You **didn't** wash the windows.
He **didn't** call me.
She **didn't** work.

We **didn't** cook.
You (all) **didn't** sweep the floor.
They **didn't** eat dinner.

exercise 13-18

Make the sentences in Exercise 13-16 negative.

1. _____

2. _____

3. _____

4. _____

5. _____

6. _____

7. _____

8. _____

9. _____

10. _____

Activities That Are Often Performed in an Office

Review the verbs in the following list. Irregular past tense forms are indicated after the slash (/):

answer (e-mail)	plan (projects)
answer (letters)	search (the Internet)
answer (the telephone)	send (a fax)/sent
attend (meetings)	take (coffee breaks)/took
check (e-mail)	type (on the keyboard)
fill (out forms)	use (the computer)
make (phone calls)/made	write (letters)/wrote
organize files	write (reports)/wrote
participate (in discussions)	

exercise   13-19

Using the verbs in the previous list, write five sentences that tell what you do or don't do at work or in an office at home. Use the present tense.

1. _____

2. _____

3. _____

4. _____

5. _____

exercise	13-20

Change the sentences in Exercise 13-19 to the past tense.

1. _____

2. _____

3. _____

4. _____

5. _____

Asking Questions

A yes-or-no question in the present tense is formed as follows:

   do/does + subject + verb

Do is used with *I, you, we,* and *they*:

   Do I need to do this?   **Do** we take the test today?
   Do you study at night?   **Do** you (all) listen to music?
                                       Do they correct their work?

Does is used with *he, she,* and *it*:

   Does she go to this school?
   Does he correct his work?
   Does the computer work?

exercise	13-21

Write yes-or-no questions in the present tense using the verbs and forms indicated. Be sure to write a question mark at the end of each question.

1. write e-mail (you) _____

2. search the Internet (he) _____

3. use the computer (she) _____

4. attend meetings (you all) _____

5. answer the telephone (they) _____

6. take coffee breaks (we) _____

Question Words

Review the words in the following list:

who
what
when
where
why
how
how much

An information question is formed as follows:

question word + *do/does* + subject + basic verb
Who do you like?
What does he do?
When do we take our coffee break?
Where do you all go after work?
Why do they have so many meetings?
How do I turn on this computer?
How much time **do** you have?

Questions with *who* and *what* do not use *do* if the question is about the *subject*. If the answer is the subject, it is formed as follows:

Who + verb   *What* + verb
Who works here?   **What** goes in this file?

exercise	13-22

Write an information question for each of the following answers. Ask the question that the italicized words answer.

1. *The telephone lists* go in that file.

   _____

2. *Mary* answers the telephone.

   _____

3. You search the Internet *in the morning*.

   _____

4. We send faxes *to the main office*.

   _____

5. They write the reports *on the computer*.

   _____

Asking Questions in the Past Tense

Yes-or-no questions in the past tense are formed as follows:

> *did* + subject + basic verb
> **Did** I do this correctly?
> **Did** you fill out the forms?
> **Did** he take the test?
> **Did** they send you a fax?

Information questions in the past tense are formed as follows:

> **question word** + *did* + subject + basic verb
> **Where did** you eat lunch?
> **When did** she go on vacation?

Questions with *who* and *what* do not use *did* if the question is about the *subject*. If the answer is the subject, it is formed as follows:

> *Who* + verb   *What* + verb
> **Who** wrote this letter?   **What** helped you learn?

exercise   13-23

Write a yes-or-no question for each of the following answers.

> EXAMPLE: I wrote a letter today.
> *Did you write a letter today?*

1. They took a long coffee break.

   _____

2. She didn't answer the telephone.

   _____

3. Mary wrote these e-mails.

   _____

4. I searched the Internet this afternoon.

   _____

5. John organized all my files.

   _____

exercise   **13-24**

Write an information question for each of the following answers. The questions should ask what the italicized words answer.

EXAMPLES: I *wrote a letter* today.   *What did you do today?*
             I wrote a letter *today.*   *When did you write a letter?*

1. *I* wrote a letter today.

_____

2. He *worked* yesterday.

_____

3. John called me *last night.*

_____

4. We ate *at home* on Monday night.

_____

5. She went home *on the bus.*

_____

Verbs Used for Shopping

Review the verbs in the following list. Irregular past tense forms are indicated after the slash (/):

ask (for advice)	read (labels)/read
ask (for help)	return
buy/bought	save (money)
cost/cost	sell/sold
examine	send/sent
find/found	show
get (a bargain)/got	sign
get (a receipt)/got	spend (money)/spent
give (money to)/gave	talk (to the manager)
hang/hung	thank (the salesclerk)
hold/held	try (on clothes)
look (at)	use (a credit card)
look (for)	wait (in line)
pay	wear/wore
pay (with cash)	write (a check)/wrote
push (a cart)	

exercise 13-25

Using verbs from the previous list, write five sentences that tell what you do when you shop at your favorite store.

1. _____
2. _____
3. _____
4. _____
5. _____

exercise 13-26

Make the sentences in Exercise 13-25 negative.

1. _____
2. _____
3. _____
4. _____
5. _____

exercise 13-27

Using past tense versions of the verbs from the previous list, write five sentences that tell what you did the last time you went shopping.

1. _____
2. _____
3. _____
4. _____
5. _____

exercise	13-28

Make the sentences in Exercise 13-27 negative.

1. _____

2. _____

3. _____

4. _____

5. _____

exercise	13-29

Write yes-or-no questions for the following answers. Use present tense verbs.

1. Yes, I return clothes that don't fit.

   _____

2. No, she doesn't always use her credit card.

   _____

3. Yes, she likes her new shoes.

   _____

4. No, we don't want these shirts.

   _____

5. No, he doesn't like to go shopping.

   _____

exercise | **13-30**

Write yes-or-no questions for the following answers. Use past tense verbs.

1. Yes, she bought a new dress.

   _____

2. Yes, he forgot to give me a receipt.

   _____

3. No, we didn't try on a lot of clothes.

   _____

4. Yes, she went shopping yesterday.

   _____

5. No, I didn't buy anything.

   _____

exercise | **13-31**

Write information questions for the following answers. Ask the question that the italicized words answer. (Be careful! Some sentences are in the present tense and others are in the past.)

1. *She* always gets a bargain.

   _____

2. We *waited in line* for thirty minutes.

   _____

3. They spent a lot of money *at that store.*

   _____

4. He always thanks *the salesclerk.*

   _____

5. I wrote the check *yesterday.*

_____

6. It cost *a hundred dollars.*

_____

Verbs Used in a Bank

Review the verbs in the following list. Irregular past tense forms are indicated after the slash (/):

apply (for a loan)
borrow (money)
bring (documents)/brought
buy (a CD)/bought
close (an account)
drive (up to the drive-up window)/drove
earn (interest)
forget/forgot
get (a PIN)/got
get (an ATM card)/got
get (cash)/got
lose/lost

make (a deposit)/made
make (an investment)/made
open (an account)
order (checks)
pay (an installment)/paid
remember (your PIN)
save (money)
speak (to the loan officer)/spoke
transfer (funds)
use (the ATM)
wait (in line)
withdraw (cash)/withdrew

exercise	13-32

Circle the most appropriate words to complete each sentence.

1. I had to order checks because I _____.

   earned interest   **lost my checkbook**   **got an ATM card**

2. She was in a hurry, so she _____.

   drove up to the drive-up window   **waited in line**   **ordered checks**

3. We brought cash because we wanted to _____.

   apply for a loan   **lose money**   **make a deposit**

4. I used my ATM card to _____.

   speak to the loan officer   **open an account**   **withdraw cash**

5. A good way to save money is to _____.

   order checks   **get a PIN**   **buy a CD**

exercise 13-33

Make the following sentences negative. Pay attention to the verb tenses.

1. They closed their account.

   _____

2. This account earns interest.

   _____

3. I got a new PIN.

   _____

4. He withdrew cash.

   _____

5. She makes a deposit every week.

   _____

exercise 13-34

Write a question for each of the following answers. Ask the question that the italicized words answer. Pay attention to the verb tenses.

1. *Yes,* I paid an installment last month.

   _____

2. *Yes,* we want to open an account.

   _____

3. She bought a CD *last week.*

   _____

4. He *applied for a loan.*

   _____

5. *They* withdraw cash.

   _____

exercise   13-35

Write five things you did at a bank this year.

1. _____

2. _____

3. _____

4. _____

5. _____

Using the Present Progressive Tense

The present progressive tense is used to tell that an activity is being performed *now*. The following expressions are used with the present progressive tense to mean *now*:

at present
currently
this week
this month
this year

The present progressive tense is formed by conjugating *be* and adding the present participle. The present participle is the basic verb + the suffix -*ing*:

| dream | **dreaming** |
| laugh | **laughing** |

• Verbs that end in -*e* drop the *e* and add -*ing*:

| dance | **dancing** |
| exercise | **exercising** |

• Verbs that end in -*ie* change the *ie* to *y* and add -*ing*:

| tie | **tying** |
| lie | **lying** |

• Verbs that end in a vowel + consonant double the consonant and add -*ing*:

| sit | **sitting** |
| stop | **stopping** |

I **am sitting** down.   We **are watching** TV.
You **are listening** to good music.   You (all) **are making** noise.
He **is sleeping**.   They **are talking** on the phone.
She **is writing** a letter.

The present progressive tense is also used to describe an activity that is planned for the near future. The following expressions are used with the present progressive tense to tell the time of a planned activity:

at 4:00	(later) this week	on Monday	tomorrow
in August	next month	soon	tonight
later	next week	this afternoon	
(later) this month	next year	this evening	

I **am leaving** tomorrow.
You **are working** this afternoon.
He **is going** home at 6:00.
She **is calling** him soon.

We **are watching** TV tonight.
You (all) **are taking** the test next week.
They **are playing** the game in October.

exercise   13-36

Change the following sentences from the present tense to the present progressive tense.

EXAMPLE: I sit down.
    I am sitting down.

1. He cashes a check.

_____

2. I withdraw money.

_____

3. They open an account.

_____

4. We apply for a loan.

_____

5. The investment earns interest.

_____

6. She gets cash from the ATM.

_____

7. I save money.

_____

8. He pays an installment on his loan.

_____

exercise	13-37

Write five sentences that tell about activities you have planned for the coming week. Use the present progressive tense.

1. _____

2. _____

3. _____

4. _____

5. _____

Verbs Used for Outdoor Activities

Review the verbs in the following list. Irregular past tense forms are indicated after the slash (/):

ask (directions)	mail (a letter)
build/built	ride (a bicycle)/rode
buy (an ice cream)/bought	run/ran
cross (the street)	see (an accident)/saw
drive (a car)/drove	sit (in the park)/sat
get (in a car)/got	stop (in an outdoor café)
get (off the bus)/got	stroll (in the city)
get (on a bus)/got	take (a walk)/took
get (out of the car)/got	take (photographs)/took
go (jogging)/went	turn (left)
go (straight ahead)/went	turn (right)
grow (flowers)/grew	visit (the zoo)
have (a picnic)/had	wait (at a red light)
hear (airplanes)/heard	wait (at a stop sign)
lie (in the sun)/lay	work (in the garden)

exercise	13-38

Fill in each blank with an activity from the previous list that best completes the sentence.

1. I never _____.

2. My best friend always _____.

3. A lot of people where I live _____ on Sundays.

4. I like to _____ every day.

5. Sometimes in the summer my friends and I _____.

exercise	13-39

Write a question for each of the following answers. Ask the question that the italicized words answer.

1. We had a picnic *in the park.*

   _____

2. *They* get off the bus here.

   _____

3. *Yes,* he took a lot of photographs.

   _____

4. *Yes,* she lay in the sun for an hour.

   _____

5. He always buys *an ice cream.*

   _____

exercise	13-40

Make each of the following sentences negative. Use the present tense.

1. She asks directions. _____

2. We turn left here. _____

3. He drives a car. _____

4. They get lost. _____

5. I go jogging. _____

exercise	13-41

Make each of the following sentences negative. Use the past tense.

1. We saw an accident. _____

2. They had a picnic. _____

3. He got on the bus. _____

4. You turned right. _____

5. She got out of the car. _____

exercise   13-42

Write in the irregular past tense forms of the following verbs.

1. be   _____

2. become   _____

3. build   _____

4. buy   _____

5. come   _____

6. do   _____

7. draw   _____

8. drink   _____

9. drive   _____

10. eat   _____

11. feel   _____

12. find   _____

13. get   _____

14. go   _____

15. grow   _____

16. have   _____

17. hear   _____

18. lie   _____

19. make   _____

20. pay   _____

21. put   _____

22. leave   _____

23. read   _____

24. ride   _____

25. run   _____

26. see   _____

27. sit   _____

28. sleep   _____

29. spend   _____

30. stand   _____

31. sweep   _____

32. take   _____

33. teach   _____

34. think   _____

35. understand   _____

36. wake up   _____

37. withdraw   _____

38. write   _____

Verbs Used for Activities in Public Places

Review the verbs in the following list. Irregular past tense forms are indicated after the slash (/):

ask (for the check in a restaurant)
buy (something from a street vendor)/bought
drink (from a water fountain)/drank
enjoy (your meal)
enter (a building)
enter (a restaurant)
enter (a train or metro station)
get (off the elevator)/got
get (on the elevator)/got
go (through revolving doors)/went

leave (a building)/left
leave (a tip)/left
leave (the station)/left
look (at the menu)
order (your meal)
pay (the waiter)/paid
push (the button)
ride (on the escalator)/rode
talk (on your cell phone)
use (the restroom)

| **exercise** | **13-43** |

Change each sentence from the past tense to the present progressive tense.

1. He got off the elevator.

   _____

2. We ordered our meal.

   _____

3. She paid the waiter.

   _____

4. We left the station.

   _____

5. They went through the revolving doors.

   _____

| **exercise** | **13-44** |

Make the following sentences negative.

1. He is leaving the building.

   _____

2. She is enjoying her meal.

   _____

3. They are riding on the escalator.

   _____

4. I am looking at the menu.

   _____

5. He's talking on his cell phone.

   _____

Make a question for each of the sentences in Exercise 13-44.

1. _____

2. _____

3. _____

4. _____

5. _____

Using the Present Perfect Tense

The verb *have* is used with the past participle to make the present perfect tense:

I **have**	we **have**
you **have**	you (all) **have**
he **has**	they **have**
she **has**	
it **has**	

The regular past participles are the same as the past tense forms:

cross	**crossed**
enter	**entered**
mail	**mailed**
walk	**walked**

Change the sentences in Exercise 13-40 to the present perfect tense.

1. _____

2. _____

3. _____

4. _____

5. _____

Verbs that are irregular in the past tense usually have an irregular past participle. Compare the verb forms in the following list. These are past participles of the irregular verbs you have already practiced.

Verb	Past Tense	Past Participle

PAST PARTICIPLE SAME AS THE BASIC VERB

become	became	become
come	came	come
cost	cost	cost
put	put	put
run	ran	run

PAST PARTICIPLE SAME AS THE PAST TENSE

bring	brought	brought
build	built	built
buy	bought	bought
feel	felt	felt
find	found	found
hang	hung	hung
have	had	had
hear	heard	heard
hold	held	held
leave	left	left
make	made	made
pay	paid	paid
read	read	read
sell	sold	sold
send	sent	sent
sit	sat	sat
sleep	slept	slept
spend	spent	spent
stand	stood	stood
sweep	swept	swept
teach	taught	taught
think	thought	thought
understand	understood	understood

PAST PARTICIPLE DIFFERENT FROM OTHER FORMS

be	was, were	been
do	did	done
draw	drew	drawn
drink	drank	drunk
drive	drove	driven
eat	ate	eaten
forget	forgot	forgotten
get	got	gotten
give	gave	given
go	went	gone
grow	grew	grown
lie	lay	lain
ride	rode	ridden
speak	spoke	spoken
take	took	taken
wake up	woke up	woken up
wear	wore	worn
withdraw	withdrew	withdrawn
write	wrote	written

exercise   **13-47**

Fill in the blank spaces with the missing forms.

Basic Verb	Past Tense	Past Participle
eat	1. _____	2. _____
3. _____	4. _____	understood
5. _____	wrote	6. _____
take	7. _____	8. _____
9. _____	10. _____	been
11. _____	taught	12. _____
come	13. _____	14. _____

One function of the present perfect tense is to tell that you are in the middle of a list of planned activities, the ones that are *already completed* and the ones that aren't completed *yet*:

I **have worked** three hours.
You **have made** one telephone call.
He **has finished** half of the problems.
She **has written** two letters.

We **have eaten** lunch.
Have you **played** any of the new games?
They **have read** almost all of the books.

The negative forms are a contraction of *have* or *has* and *not*:

I **haven't finished** the project.
You **haven't done** your homework.
He **hasn't watched** this movie.
She **hasn't come** in yet.

We **haven't eaten** dinner.
You (all) **haven't ridden** in my new car.
They **haven't paid** the bill.

exercise   **13-48**

Change the following sentences from the past tense to the present perfect tense.

1. I didn't eat dinner.

   _____

2. She didn't leave the station.

   _____

3. We didn't look at the menu.

   _____

4. He didn't order his lunch.

   _____

5. She paid the waiter.

_____

6. We didn't buy anything from a street vendor.

_____

7. I asked for the check.

_____

Verbs Used for Leisure Activities

Review the verbs in the following list. Irregular past tense forms appear after the first slash (/); irregular past participles appear after the second slash:

begin (the game)/began/begun
catch (the ball)/caught/caught
compete
dance
go (for a walk)/went/gone
go (to a concert)/went/gone
go (to the movies)/went/gone
go (to the theater)/went/gone
have (a drink with someone)/had/had
have (a party)/had/had
have (coffee with someone)/had/had
have (dinner)/had/had
have (lunch)/had/had
hit (the ball)/hit/hit
kick (the ball)

listen (to music)
listen (to the radio)
lose (the game)/lost/lost
participate (in a sport)
play (a game)
play (an instrument)
see (a movie)/saw/seen
sing/sang/sung
start (the game)
swim/swam/swum
throw (the ball)/threw/thrown
watch (a game)
watch (TV)
win the game/won/won

exercise   13-49

Change the sentences from the present tense to the present progressive tense.

1. The game begins. _____

2. He swims. _____

3. They win. _____

4. She throws the ball. _____

5. We sing together. _____

6. I go to the movies. _____

exercise	13-50

Write a yes-or-no question for each of your answers to Exercise 13-49.

1. _____

2. _____

3. _____

4. _____

5. _____

6. _____

exercise	13-51

Make the following sentences negative.

1. He has hit the ball. _____

2. I have seen that movie. _____

3. She has had lunch with him. _____

4. We have sung that song. _____

5. They have danced together before. _____

Asking Questions with *Have*

Questions in the present perfect tense put *have* or *has* between the subject of the sentence and the past participle:

Have I **danced** with you before?   **Have** we **lost** the game?
Have you **seen** the play?   **Have** you (all) **eaten**?
Has he **played** yet?   **Have** they **won** the game?
Has she **gone** for a walk?

exercise	13-52

Write yes-or-no questions for the sentences in Exercise 13-51.

1. _____

2. _____

3. _____

4. _____

5. _____

exercise   13-53

Choose five items from the list of leisure activities and write a sentence for each, telling whether you have or haven't done that activity this month.

1. _____

2. _____

3. _____

4. _____

5. _____

exercise   13-54

Choose five items from the list of leisure activities that you are planning to do, and write a sentence for each in the present progressive tense, telling when you plan to do it.

1. _____

2. _____

3. _____

4. _____

5. _____

Verbs Used for Cooking

Review the verbs in the following list. Irregular past tense forms are indicated after the first slash (/); irregular past participles are indicated after the second slash:

add	grill
arrange	ice (a cake)
bake	marinate
barbecue	microwave
beat/beat/beaten	mix
blend	peel
boil	pour

break (an egg)/broke/broken   process
broil   refrigerate
buy (ingredients)/bought/bought   remove (from oven)
chill   remove (from pan)
chop   sauté
cook   separate (an egg)
cut (into pieces)/cut/cut   simmer
decorate   slice
dice   spread/spread/spread
freeze/froze/frozen   sprinkle
frost (a cake)   stir
fry   strain
garnish   whip

exercise   13-55

*Write the number 1 next to each activity below that involves **preparation before cooking**. Write the number 2 next to each activity that involves **cooking**. Write the number 3 next to each activity that occurs **before serving**.*

1. _____ arrange

2. _____ bake

3. _____ break an egg

4. _____ decorate

5. _____ fry

6. _____ garnish

7. _____ ice a cake

8. _____ marinate

9. _____ mix

10. _____ process

11. _____ sauté

12. _____ simmer

exercise   **13-56**

Change the following sentences from the present tense to the past tense.

1. I add tomatoes to the sauce.

   _____

2. She ices and decorates the cakes in the morning.

   _____

3. He whips the cream.

   _____

4. They cook for a lot of people.

   _____

5. We grill the fish outside.

   _____

exercise   **13-57**

Write a yes-or-no question for each of your answers to Exercise 13-56.

1. _____

2. _____

3. _____

4. _____

5. _____

exercise   **13-58**

Change the following sentences from the past tense to the present perfect tense.

1. We barbecued the chicken.

   _____

2. She removed the pan from the oven.

   _____

3. He arranged the salad on the plates.

    _____

4. I peeled the potatoes.

    _____

5. They spread butter on the bread.

    _____

Giving Directions

The basic verb is used to give commands:

> **Come** here.
> **Bring** me a drink.
> **Go** away.
> **Turn** on the light.

Negative commands are formed by adding *don't* before the verb:

> **Don't come.**
> **Don't bring** me anything.
> **Don't go.**
> **Don't turn** on the light.

exercise   13-59

Circle the verbs that best complete the sentences to form instructions in the kitchen.

1. _____ the tomatoes.

    Ice   **Break**   **Slice**   **Whip**

2. _____ the cake.

    Barbecue   **Ice**   **Fry**   **Strain**

3. _____ the pan from the oven.

    Remove   **Chop**   **Spread**   **Chill**

4. _____ butter on the bread.

    Spread   **Boil**   **Bake**   **Peel**

5. _____ the champagne.

    Dice   **Whip**   **Chill**   **Boil**

6. _____ the eggs into the bowl.

    Barbecue   **Freeze**   **Ice**   **Break**

7. _____ a loaf of bread.

    Beat   **Boil**   **Bake**   **Peel**

8. _____ water for the tea.

    Boil   **Fry**   **Sauté**   **Decorate**

exercise   13-60

Change the verbs in Exercise 13-59 to the present progressive tense to write complete sentences that tell what you are in the middle of doing in the kitchen.

1. _____

2. _____

3. _____

4. _____

5. _____

6. _____

7. _____

8. _____

PART IV

ADVERBS

Adverbs are the mechanical tools in our vocabulary. They include words that help us give facts about the states or actions described by verbs. Adverbs enable us to tell where, when, or how often something exists or takes place. For example, "The party is *here*." "The party is *tonight*." "They have a party *every night*." Adverbs enable us to tell how an activity is done, for example, "She drives *very carefully*."

Adverbs are important for understanding and giving information about events and activities. Be accurate with adverbs!

Adverbs of Place, Time, and Frequency

Adverbs of Place

Certain adverbs answer the question *Where?* Review the adverbs in the following list:

ahead	in
away	inside
below	nearby
close	nowhere
down	out
downstairs	outside
everywhere	there
far away	up
here	upstairs

exercise 14-1

Match each adverb in the left column with its opposite in the right column.

_____ 1. downstairs   a. away

_____ 2. here   b. far away

_____ 3. inside   c. here

_____ 4. close by/nearby   d. nowhere

_____ 5. there   e. outside

_____ 6. everywhere   f. out

_____ 7. up   g. upstairs

_____ 8. in   h. down

An adverb of place after the verb *be* tells the location of a person, place, or thing:

> We are **here**.
> The girls are **inside**.
> Springfield is **nearby**.
> The books are **upstairs**.

exercise   14-2

Write the name of a person, a place, or a thing that is in each of the following locations in relation to where you are now.

1. here   _____

2. there   _____

3. away   _____

4. inside   _____

5. outside   _____

6. nearby   _____

7. far away   _____

8. everywhere   _____

An adverb of place after a verb of movement indicates where a person or thing goes.

exercise   14-3

Fill in each blank with the adverb described.

1. I want to go (to that place) _____.

2. Please move your car (to where I am) _____.

3. Let's drive (to the other side of town) _____.

4. I'm going (to the interior of the house) _____.

5. She's (not far away) _____.

6. He climbed (to the top of the ladder) _____.

7. He ran (to the floor below) _____.

8. She walked (to where the fresh air is) _____.

Using Prepositional Phrases as Adverbs to Indicate Location

Review the expressions in the following list:

Expressions with *in*	Expressions with *on*	Expressions with *at*
in a building	on a balcony	at a place
in a car	on a bicycle	at a restaurant
in a city	on a bus	at an address
in a corner (inside)	on a corner (outside)	at church
in a house	on a deck	at home
in a private airplane	on a hard chair	at school
in a room	on a horse	at the airport
in a small boat	on a motorcycle	at the beach
in a soft chair	on a patio	at the library
in an office	on a ship	at the office
in bed	on a street	at the zoo
in jail	on a train	at work
in the bathtub	on foot	
in the country	on the floor	
in the garden	on the fourth floor	
in the hospital	on the left side	
in the kitchen	on the metro	
in the middle of a place	on the right side	
in the mountains		
in the water		
in town		

exercise   14-4

Fill in each blank with the most appropriate expression from the previous list.

1. We don't live in the city; we live _____.

2. She visited a farm and rode _____.

3. A friend of mine drives to work _____.

4. He lives _____ of that building.

5. They put the new table _____.

6. She committed a crime, and now she is _____.

7. My cousin had an operation and is still _____.

8. We put the grill and the outdoor furniture _____.

9. My daughter isn't at home now; she's studying _____.

10. I don't drive, so I ride to work _____.

Location and Direction

North	Toronto is in the north of North America.
	Canada is north of the United States.
	We are going north for our summer vacation.
South	Miami is in the south of Florida.
	Florida is south of Georgia.
	The birds fly south in the winter.
East	Washington, D.C., is in the east of the United States.
	Washington, D.C., is east of Virginia.
	The plane is flying east.
West	California is in the west of the United States.
	Texas is west of Louisiana.
	The pioneers moved west.

exercise   14-5

Answer the following questions using words from the list of directions. Use complete sentences.

1. Where do you live?

   _____

2. Where is your home in relation to New York?

   _____

3. Where are you going on your next vacation?

   _____

4. Where is that in relation to where you live?

   _____

5. Where is Mexico?

   _____

Adverbs of Time

Certain adverbs answer the question *When?* Review the adverbs in the following list:

Past	Present	Future
a few days ago	already	afterward
a month ago	no longer	Friday night
a week ago	not yet	later
a year ago	now	next month
before	6:00	next October
last month	still	next Thursday
last night	this afternoon	next week
last Tuesday	this evening	next year
last week	this morning	soon
last year	today	then
recently	tonight	this Friday
ten years ago		tomorrow
then		tomorrow morning
this afternoon		Wednesday afternoon
this morning		
yesterday		

exercise 14-6

Fill in each blank with a word or expression from the previous list.

Assume that today is Sunday, the seventh of August 2005. It is 4:00 P.M.

1. _____ was the sixth of August.

2. _____ is the eighth of August.

3. September is _____.

4. July was _____.

5. The twelfth of August is _____.

6. February 2006 is _____.

7. The seventh of August 1995 was _____.

8. I ate breakfast _____.

9. I will eat dinner _____.

10. My birthday is _____.

Using Prepositional Phrases as Adverbs to Indicate Time

Review the expressions in the following list:

Expressions with *in*	Expressions with *on*	Expressions with *at*
in five years	on holidays	at 5:45 P.M.
in March	on July 15	at midnight
in 1995	on my birthday	at night
in ten minutes	on Tuesday	at noon
in the afternoon	on Tuesdays	at 10:00
in the evening	on weekdays	at 3:30
in the middle of the day	on weekends	at 2:30 A.M.
in the middle of the month		
in the middle of the year		
in the morning		
in 2010		

exercise   14-7

Fill in the blanks with the most appropriate expression from the previous list.

1. It is 3:00. I am leaving in thirty minutes. I am leaving _____.

2. She has classes every Monday through Friday. She has classes _____.

3. I am going on vacation the month after February. I am going on vacation _____.

4. It is 2005. He is going to finish school five years from now. He is going to finish

   _____.

5. We will go to work after we get up tomorrow. We will go to work _____.

Relative Times

before
after
early
late

My appointment is at 3:00. It is **before** 4:00.
Tuesday is **before** Wednesday.
I get off work at 5:00. It is **after** 4:00.
Thursday is **after** Wednesday.
Class begins at 6:00 A.M. It is **early** in the morning.
I get home at 10:00 P.M. It is **late** in the evening.
Class begins at 9:00. If you come at 8:30, you are **early**.
If you come at 9:30, you are **late**.

exercise	14-8

Match the expressions in the left column with those in the right column.

_____ 1. 11:30 P.M.	a. after Friday
_____ 2. 5:00 A.M.	b. before Tuesday
_____ 3. after the event has started	c. early
_____ 4. at noon	d. early in the morning
_____ 5. before the event starts	e. early in the year
_____ 6. in January	f. in June
_____ 7. in November	g. in the middle of the day
_____ 8. in the middle of the month	h. late
_____ 9. in the middle of the year	i. late at night
_____ 10. on Monday	j. late in the year
_____ 11. on Saturday	k. on the fifteenth

Adverbs of Frequency

Certain adverbs can answer the question *How often?* Review the adverbs in the following list:

always	often
frequently	rarely
hardly ever	seldom
never	sometimes
occasionally	usually

exercise	14-9

Answer the following questions using adverbs from the previous list. Put the adverb before the verb. Use complete sentences.

1. How often do you ride the metro?

   _____

2. How often does your best friend call you on the telephone?

   _____

3. How often do you sleep eight hours a night?

_____

4. How often do your neighbors have parties?

_____

Certain other expressions indicate how often an activity is performed. These expressions are placed after the verb:

all the time
every day
every so often
once a week
three times a year
twice a month

| exercise | 14-10 |

Answer the following questions using adverbs from the previous list. Use complete sentences.

1. What do you do every so often?

_____

2. How often do you sit down to eat?

_____

3. How often do you go on vacation?

_____

4. What do you do every day?

_____

5. What special occasion happens once a year?

_____

Adverbs of Manner

Certain adverbs indicate how an action is performed.

Forming Adverbs from Adjectives

Many adverbs of manner are formed by adding -ly to an adjective:

glad	**gladly**
honest	**honestly**
nice	**nicely**

Adverbs that end in -y change the y to i and then add -ly:

easy	**easily**
happy	**happily**
noisy	**noisily**

Adverbs that end in -ic add -ally:

enthusiastic	**enthusiastically**
tragic	**tragically**

Adverbs that end in -ble drop the e and add -y:

comfortable	**comfortably**
humble	**humbly**

Certain adverbs are the same as the corresponding adjective:

early	**early**
fast	**fast**
hard	**hard**
late	**late**

The adverb for *good* is *well*.

exercise   15-1

Write the adverbs that correspond to the following adjectives.

1. active   _____

2. aggressive   _____

3. bad   _____

4. bitter   _____

5. brave   _____

6. careful   _____

7. cautious   _____

8. charming   _____

9. cheap   _____

10. cheerful   _____

11. civil   _____

12. competent   _____

13. considerate   _____

14. creative   _____

15. efficient   _____

16. faithful   _____

17. fortunate   _____

18. generous   _____

19. glad   _____

20. imaginative   _____

21. interesting   _____

22. kind   _____

23. loud   _____

24. modest   _____

25. natural   _____

26. nervous   _____

27. nice   _____

28. patient   _____

29. pleasant   _____

30. polite   _____

31. proper   _____

32. proud   _____

33. quiet   _____

34. reverent   _____

35. secure   _____

36. selfish   _____

37. serious   _____

38. sincere   _____

39. skillful   _____

40. slow   _____

41. soft   _____

42. successful _____

43. sweet   _____

44. tactful   _____

45. truthful   _____

46. weak   _____

exercise   15-2

Write the adverbs that correspond to the following adjectives.

1. capable   _____

2. comfortable   _____

3. easy   _____

4. energetic   _____

5. enthusiastic   _____

6. fast   _____

7. good   _____

8. humble   _____

9. happy   _____

10. noisy   _____

11. reasonable   _____

12. responsible   _____

13. tragic   _____

exercise   15-3

Circle the most appropriate adverb to fill in the blank.

1. He went into the burning house and saved the child. He acted _____.

   tragically   **easily**   **bravely**   **sweetly**

2. She always came to work and completed her assignments on time. She acted _____.

   responsibly   **humbly**   **generously**   **easily**

3. He solved all the math problems right away. He solved them _____.

   easily   **nicely**   **slowly**   **nervously**

4. _____, nobody was injured in the accident.

   Successfully   **Fortunately**   **Proudly**   **Skillfully**

5. That store is great; it always accepts returned items _____.

   selfishly   **actively**   **cheaply**   **cheerfully**

6. The customs agent _____ examined all the packages so as not to do any damage.

   noisily   **carefully**   **aggressively**   **enthusiastically**

7. She _____ accepted the invitation.

   tragically   **truthfully**   **imaginatively**   **gladly**

8. He failed the course because his papers were written very _____.

   badly   **cautiously**   **well**   **capably**

9. She's an artist; everything she does is done _____.

   bitterly   **charmingly**   **creatively**   **quietly**

10. He's a wonderful teacher who answers all your questions very _____.

    aggressively   **actively**   **cheaply**   **patiently**

exercise	15-4

Write a sentence for each of five different people, telling how each one performs a particular activity.

   EXAMPLE: *My friend Jim works quickly.*

1. _____

2. _____

3. _____

4. _____

5. _____

Comparing Adverbs

Adverbs of manner can be compared by using *more* + **adverb** + *than*:

He argues **more** aggressively **than** the other lawyer.
She writes **more** creatively **than** the other students.

exercise	15-5

Write a sentence for each of the following comparisons usng the cues given in parentheses.

1. John drives at fifty-five miles per hour. Mary drives at sixty-five miles per hour. How does John drive? (slowly)

    _____

2. Susan makes only a few mistakes. Janet makes a lot of mistakes. How does Susan work? (carefully)

    _____

3. David makes a lot of noise when he plays. Charles doesn't make noise. How does Charles play? (quietly)

    _____

Certain adverbs have different forms:

badly	**worse than**
early	**earlier than**
fast	**faster than**
hard	**harder than**
late	**later than**
well	**better than**

A negative comparison is made by using *not* + **verb** + *as* + **adverb** + *as*:

> We do**n't** play **as** skillfully **as** the other team.
> She does**n't** play the piano **as** well **as** you.
> He does**n't** run **as** fast **as** his brother.

exercise	15-6

Compare the actions of each of the people you described in Exercise 15-4 with those of another person.

1. _____

2. _____

3. _____

4. _____

5. _____

exercise　　15-7

Look at Exercise 15-5 and answer the following questions using a negative comparison.

1. How does Mary drive in comparison with John?

   _____

2. How does Janet work in comparison with Susan?

   _____

3. How does David play in comparison with Charles?

   _____

exercise　　15-8

Complete the following chart by writing positive comparisons for the negative examples and negative comparisons for the positive ones.

Positive	Negative
1. more slowly than	_____
2. _____	not as fast as
3. more quietly than	_____
4. _____	not as well as
5. more energetically than	_____
6. _____	not as early as
7. more efficiently than	_____
8. _____	not as patiently as
9. harder than	_____
10. _____	not as seriously as
11. later than	_____
12. _____	not as sweetly as

exercise   **15-9**

Write five sentences that tell what activities you perform at home or at work and how you do each one.

1. _____

2. _____

3. _____

4. _____

5. _____

exercise   **15-10**

Compare the way you do the activities you described in Exercise 15-9 with the way someone else does them.

1. _____

2. _____

3. _____

4. _____

5. _____

Unit 16

Adverbs That Modify

Adverbs That Modify Verbs

Certain adverbs tell how intensely an action is performed:

hardly/scarcely	=	almost not at all
a little/very little	=	some
well enough	=	adequately
really/well	=	very well

The adverbs *hardly, scarcely,* and *really* are placed before the verb they modify:

My car **hardly** runs.

She **scarcely** visits us.

The machine **really** helps.

exercise   16-1

Fill in each blank with the appropriate adverb of intensity.

1. Their new sports car is powerful. It _____ moves.

2. His grandmother is in a wheelchair because she _____ walks.

3. Now that he has studied a year in Mexico, he _____ understands Spanish.

4. Her new boyfriend is so quiet. He _____ said a word at the party.

The adverbs *a little, very little, well enough,* and *well* are placed after the verb they modify:

> She sings **a little**.
> He plays **well enough**.
> They dance **well**.

exercise   16-2

Fill in each blank with the appropriate adverb of intensity.

1. The new employee is not creative, but he's responsible. He works

   _____.

2. She is a great teacher. She is understanding, and she explains the lessons

   _____.

3. I'm not an expert, but I can dance _____.

4. He isn't a great player, but he plays _____.

5. They are excellent speakers. They speak _____.

exercise   16-3

Answer each of the following questions in a complete sentence.

1. What do you hardly do at all?

   _____

2. What do you do a little?

   _____

3. How hard do you work every day?

   _____

4. Who or what really helps you?

   _____

5. What do you do well enough?

   _____

Adverbs That Modify Adjectives and Other Adverbs

Certain adverbs give strength to an adjective:

not at all < fairly < pretty < rather/quite < very < extremely < too

He is **not at all** shy. (He's the opposite of shy.)
He is **fairly** nice. (He's a little bit nice.)
She is **pretty** strict. (She's not a dictator but she maintains discipline.)
We are **rather** tired. (We need a rest before we can do anything else.)
They are **very** expensive. (They cost more than I would like to pay.)
They are **extremely** expensive. (They cost a lot more than I would like to pay.)
They are **too** expensive. (They cost so much that I will not buy them.)

exercise   16-4

Choose the best adverb from the previous list to fill in each blank.

1. When I got home from work I was _____ tired, so I sat down to rest for a while.

2. I'm not going to the party tonight because I am _____ tired.

3. After hiking all day, I was _____ tired.

4. I didn't sleep well last night, so I was _____ tired when I got up.

5. I took a nap when I got home, so I was _____ tired when my guests arrived.

exercise   16-5

Answer each question using adverbs from the previous list to modify the adjectives.

1. What do you do when you are extremely happy?

    _____

2. What do you do if your friends are too busy to go out?

    _____

3. What do your friends do if you are pretty sick?

    _____

4. What does your boss do if you arrive rather late?

    _____

5. What did you think of the last movie you saw?

    _____

6. What is the weather like today?

    _____

7. Are these exercises hard?

    _____

8. What is not at all easy for you?

    _____

A comparison can be made with an adjective by adding the adverb *much* before the comparative form:

> He is **much** taller than I am.
> She is **much** quieter than she was before.
> This movie is **much** better than the other one.
> She's feeling **much** worse.
> She is **much** more aggressive than her sister.

exercise   16-6

Using the cues in parentheses, write sentences that compare the following pairs.

1. Sara is four feet ten inches tall. Her brother is six feet two inches tall. (short)

_____

2. Jackie smiles and talks to everybody. Susan doesn't talk to anybody. (friendly)

_____

3. Joe cleans the house, cooks, and washes the dishes. Jim helps only a little around the house. (helpful)

_____

4. Mary plays volleyball, basketball, softball, soccer, and tennis. Her sister sometimes plays tennis. (athletic)

_____

5. Patricia's baby weighed five pounds. Valerie's baby weighed ten pounds. (small)

_____

The adverbs *fairly, pretty, rather, quite, very, extremely,* and *too* can also modify other adverbs:

> I walk **fairly** fast.
> She reads **pretty** well.
> He works **rather** slowly.
> He drives **very** carefully.
> They work **extremely** hard.
> She speaks **too** softly. (Nobody can hear her.)

exercise   16-7

Use the adverbs from the previous list to answer the following questions about yourself.

1. How well do you cook?

   _____

2. How hard do you work?

   _____

3. What do you do rather quickly?

   _____

4. Do you sleep well?

   _____

5. What do you do too slowly?

   _____

exercise   16-8

Use the adverbs from the previous list to answer the following questions about someone you know.

1. How well does he or she cook?

   _____

2. How hard does he or she work?

   _____

3. What does he or she do rather quickly?

   _____

4. Does he or she drive well?

   _____

5. How hard does he or she work?

   _____

PART V

ENGLISH IN THE TWENTY-FIRST CENTURY: TECHNOLOGY

General Vocabulary for Technology

Here is the basic vocabulary of computer technology.

Nouns

The Computer

personal computer/PC: *a machine used for preparing and storing documents, communicating and getting information through the Internet, and providing entertainment*

desktop: *a full-size computer that is installed and used on a desk or table*

laptop: *a portable computer of a size that can be set on one's lap*

notebook: *a portable computer, smaller than a laptop*

palmtop: *a small, wireless computer that can be held in the hand*

tablet: *a touch-screen wireless minicomputer that enables the user to watch videos, play games, read publications, and access the Internet*

hard drive/hard disk drive/HDD: *a basic part of the computer that stores its important information, such as programs and data files*

hardware: *the computer and the physical accessories necessary for its functioning*

program: *a set of instructions that enable a computer to perform a specific task*

software: *the programs installed on the hardware that tell the computer what to do*

operating system/OS: *a large collection of programs that controls operations of the computer; the basic software that allows the user and the computer to interact and the computer's hardware and software applications to communicate*

application/app: *software added to the operating system that enables a specific task to be performed*

device: *a machine used to perform one or several tasks*

gadget/gizmo: *a device*

USB port: *a small connector in the computer that allows a device or accessory to connect to the computer*

accessories: *items that help you or may be necessary for using your equipment*

screen: *the lighted panel that displays your work or other information on the computer*

mouse: *a pointing device that is held under one of the computer user's hands and is used to move the cursor on the computer screen*

touch pad: *a small device built into laptop computers that functions as an alternative to a mouse*

cursor: *an indicator on a computer screen that shows where a user can enter text*

keyboard: *a device with letters, numbers, and other instructional buttons that enables you to prepare a document or perform other tasks on the computer; usually used in connection with a mouse or touch pad.*

keypad: *a type of keyboard that may have specialized tasks when used with machines other than a computer*

compact disc/CD: *a round, flat unit (disc), 4¾ inches in diameter, which contains digital information you can access with your computer*

rewritable disc/CD-R/DVD-R: *a CD or DVD on which you can save and store your work or other information from the computer*

USB flash drive: *a small device on which you can save and store large amounts of your work or other information from the computer; it is portable and enables you to continue working on or reading your documents on another computer*

printer: *a machine connected to your computer that enables you to reproduce on paper your work or other material found on the computer*

ink-jet: *a type of printer that uses ink to reproduce images on paper*

cartridge: *the case holding ink for an ink-jet printer or toner for a laser printer or copier*

laser: *a type of printer that is faster than an ink-jet and is good for making a large number of copies*

toner: *a powder used instead of ink in a laser printer*

scanner: *a machine connected to your computer that can reproduce an exact image in digital form and allow you to view and store it on your computer*

copier: *a machine that can make photocopies of images or documents*

earphones: *devices you place in your ears that enable you to privately hear music or other audio material from a computer or other machine*

headset: *a device that you place over your ears as a substitute for earphones*

I prefer to use a **desktop** computer, but I take a **notebook** with me when I travel.

Manufacturers of **operating systems** usually introduce new programs every three or four years.

Can you use a **CD** with your new **laptop**?

It's a good idea to save your work on a **CD** or a **USB flash drive**.

Sometimes it's hard to choose between an **ink-jet printer** and a **laser printer**.

Do you prefer to use a **headset** or **earphones**?

| exercise | 17-1 |

Choose the most appropriate word or words to complete each sentence.

1. One way to save work you have done on a computer is with a _____.

   headset   **laser**   **USB flash drive**   **cursor**

2. If your laser printer starts printing lighter images, you probably need _____.

   toner   **an ink cartridge**   **a new keypad**   **a scanner**

3. A convenient way to do word processing while you are traveling is to take with you

   a _____.

   compact disc   **laptop**   **desktop computer**   **tablet**

4. You probably need a new computer if your _____ is destroyed.

   printer   **scanner**   **hard drive**   **USB flash drive**

5. If you want to write a letter using a computer, you need to know how to use the _____.

   headset   **scanner**   **keyboard**   **laser**

| exercise | 17-2 |

Do you use a computer? Do you prefer a desktop or a laptop? What operating system do you use? What accessories do you use with your computer?

_____

_____

The Internet

The **Internet** is the global system of interconnected computer networks that allows access to the World Wide Web and a wide range of other resources.

World Wide Web/the Web/www: *a part of the universe of information that is accessible through the Internet; the Web has a body of software with a set of guidelines that allows you to get information or contribute to the information available*

cyberspace: *the nonphysical area created and inhabited by the Internet*

cable: *a system of underground wires that enables access to Internet and television services*

broadband: *a high-speed Internet system*

modem: *a device used to connect to the Internet using either cable or telephone lines*

router: *a device that links a computer to a network, thus enabling Internet service*

Bluetooth: *a wireless system built into certain devices that provides a secure way to connect and exchange information between them; Bluetooth exists in many products, such as telephones, games, watches, some high-definition (HD) headsets, modems, and watches. HD headsets offer improved, high-definition sound quality and have Bluetooth, as do certain watches, which work with telephones to display caller ID (so you don't have to get out your cell phone to see who's calling)*

Wi-Fi: *a wireless technology that enables network access*

hot spot: *a Wi-Fi connection to the Internet*

You can find the answer to many questions on the **Internet**, but it's important to remember that not everything you read there is correct.

Do you have a **cable** connection to the Web where you live, or do you depend on **Wi-Fi**?

More and more **hot spots** are being made available worldwide.

exercise	17-3

Circle the most appropriate word or words to complete each sentence.

1. The Internet is also known as _____.

   Bluetooth   **Wi-Fi**   **the Web**   **cable**

2. To connect your computer to the Internet, you need _____.

   Bluetooth   **broadband**   **a modem**   **cyberspace**

3. The Internet is accessible _____.

   only in the   **only in highly**   **worldwide**   **only to educated**
   United States   **developed countries**   **people**

4. A hot spot refers to _____.

   cyberspace   **cable**   **a router**   **Wi-Fi**
                                                     connection

Using the Computer

To use the computer as a word processor, you need to purchase and install an operating system and connect the computer to an electrical outlet. You can use a laptop computer with a battery that can be recharged in an electrical outlet.

To use a printer, you need to connect it to your computer and to an electrical outlet, then follow the instructions for installing it.

To use the Internet, you need to either subscribe to a cable service or find a Wi-Fi hot spot.

Adjectives

analog: *refers to the traditional way of recording, storing, and transmitting sound and information*

digital: *refers to a way of recording and storing sound that is more suited to computers*

embedded: *built into a device*

smart: *capable of making adjustments that resemble human decisions, especially in response to changing circumstances; some examples are smartphone, smart card, SMART Board*

wireless: *having the capability of functioning without the use of a cable*

touch screen: *a feature on certain computers that enables you to give commands and enter information by touching the screen with your fingers instead of using a mouse*

Verbs

plug in: *to connect a cord to an electrical outlet or a wire to a device or machine*

key in: *to put information into a computer by using a keyboard*

store: *to save information on the computer for future viewing*

install: *to set up a machine so that it will function*

enable: *to make possible*

download: *to receive information from the Internet on your computer*

upload: *to add information to an Internet site*

copy: *to reproduce a document*

save: *to make sure your work or other information remains available in the computer for future viewing and editing*

print: *to reproduce on paper your work or other information on the computer*

Our new teacher uses the **SMART Board** to help us learn geography.

If your computer isn't working, the first thing to do is make sure that it is **plugged in**.

When you buy a **printer**, you need to follow the directions for **installing** it in your computer.

The professor required his students to **download** a lot of information from the **Internet**.

exercise 17-4

Circle the most appropriate word or words to complete each sentence.

1. The traditional way of storing sound is with _____ device.

   an embedded   **an analog**   **a smart**   **a wireless**

2. On some computers, you can use a _____ to give commands.

   digital phone   **touch screen**   **Wi-Fi**   **scanner**

3. If you do not want to lose work you have done on a computer, you need to _____ it.

   copy   **print**   **install**   **save**

4. Getting information from the Internet on your computer screen is called _____.

   uploading   **installing**   **downloading**   **keying in**

Contacting Other People: The Technology of Communications

The Telephone

The telephone, or phone, is a device that transmits and receives sound, most commonly the human voice. It allows two people separated by large distances to talk to each other.

Types

corded/landline: *a telephone connected by a pair of wires to a telephone network*

cordless: *a telephone that has a portable handset that communicates by radio with a base station that is connected by wire to the telephone network; it does not function when it is too far from the base station*

mobile/cell: *a portable telephone that communicates with the telephone network by radio; it usually functions over a wide area, within a country, and sometimes even internationally*

smartphone: *a mobile phone with an embedded computer that enables you to perform a number of tasks in addition to speaking and listening*

Applications/Apps

Apps that are available on some mobile phones enable the following operations:

text messaging: *sending a written message that will appear on the telephone screen of the person you are contacting*

using the Internet: *finding information on the Internet*

using e-mail: *sending a written message that will appear on the computer of the person you are contacting*

navigating: *getting directions to a different location*

taking photographs: *using a digital camera that is built into the telephone*

making a video: *using a digital video camera that is built into the telephone*

face-to-face talking: *using a device that enables you to see the person you are talking to*

listening to music: *using a device that allows you to download music to your telephone and listen to it through earphones*

Telephone Parts

handset: *the device that you hold in your hand and place next to your ear and close to your mouth so that you can listen and talk*

microphone: *a device built into the handset where you direct your voice*

earphone: *a device that reproduces the voice of the other person*

ringer: *a device that makes a sound so that you know when a call is coming in*

ringtone: *the sound or music made by the ringer*

vibrate: *an option on a cell phone that produces motion so that you know when a call is coming in when you have the ringer turned off*

keypad: *a grid of numbers, letters, and symbols that enables you to enter the telephone number of the person you want to contact, usually located on the handset; it may be in the form of buttons to push or a touch screen*

Many people have decided to use only a **cell phone** instead of having a **landline**.

It is dangerous to talk on a **cell phone** or send a **text message** while you are driving a car.

The **ringer** on his **cell phone** makes a musical sound.

When you're at the movies, you should turn off the **ringer** on your **cell phone**, and put it on vibrate if you're expecting a call.

exercise 18-1

Choose the most appropriate word or words to complete the following sentences.

1. Your telephone is equipped with _____ so that you can hear the person on the line.

   a handset   **an earphone**   **a microphone**   **a keypad**

2. Your telephone is equipped with _____ so that you know when a call is coming in.

   a keypad   **a microphone**   **an earphone**   **a ringer**

3. A telephone cannot be used for _____.

   printing a document   **taking pictures**   **sending a written message**   **checking your e-mail**

4. You can use a _____ when you go for a walk in your neighborhood.

   cell phone   **cordless phone**   **landline**   **all of the previous answers**

Using the Telephone

For a telephone to function, it must be connected to a communication service provided by one of a number of private companies that do business in particular geographic areas. In some countries, this service is provided by the government. Each company has its own set of optional services and payment scales. Customers are usually billed monthly for these services.

telephone call: *a communication from one telephone to another*

area code: *a three-digit number (in the United States—it may be different in other countries) assigned to a limited area, which can include part of a city, an entire city, an area of a state, or, if it has a small population, an entire state*

country code: *a two-digit number assigned to a country for use in international calls*

telephone number: *a person's area code, followed by a seven-digit number (in the United States) assigned by a telephone service to that person; your telephone number identifies you in the telephone system*

operator: *an employee of a telephone company who helps make connections*

pay phone: *a public telephone from which you can call someone after inserting coins or a credit card, or entering the number from a calling card*

calling card: *a small card that you can buy in advance that enables you to make calls from a pay phone or from your personal phone when you enter the number or code printed on the card*

Types of Calls

local: *a call to or from someone who lives within your area code*

long-distance: *a call to or from someone who lives outside your area code, but in the same country*

international: *a call to or from someone in a different country*

operator-assisted: *a call, usually international, made with the assistance of an operator*

direct dial: *an international call made by entering on a keypad the digits 011 (calling from the United States), followed by the country code, the area code, and the telephone number of the person you are calling*

conference: *a call between more than two telephones, allowing a group conversation*

Telephone Options

caller ID: *the telephone number (identification) of the person who is calling you; if you have this option, this number appears on your telephone before you answer a call*

voice mail: *a service that answers your telephone when you are unable to and allows the caller to leave a message*

speakerphone: *a device built into some telephones that allows you to listen and speak from the same room without holding the handset up to your face*

call waiting: *a service that alerts you during a call to inform you that another person is calling you at that moment and that you can choose to accept that call and ask the current caller to wait for a few moments*

Making Calls to a Business

When you make a call to a business, a machine-recorded voice often answers and asks you to choose from a number of **menu options** by keying in a number on your telephone. The options usually include different departments or individuals at the business. After choosing the department you wish to speak to, you may then be asked to wait **on hold** until someone is able to speak to you. Sometimes the information you want can be provided by the machine. In other cases, you may have to request the aid of an **agent**. Very often, you are told that your questions to the business can be answered **online** (through the Internet).

The Fax Machine

fax machine: *a machine that enables you to send a document over a telephone line; the machine copies the document and sends it electronically to its destination*

fax: *the document you send through a fax machine*

fax: *a verb that means to send a fax*

fax server: *a computerized system that receives and stores incoming faxes electronically*

She wanted to keep her **telephone number** a secret but found out that it was on the **Internet**.

I couldn't get my call to go through, so I got the **operator** to place it for me.

If he doesn't answer the phone, leave a message on his **voice mail**.

It's frustrating when you are put **on hold** and have to wait a long time for someone to answer.

---

exercise   18-2

What kind of telephone do you have? What apps does it have? Make a list here.

_____

_____

_____

---

exercise   18-3

Choose the most appropriate word or words to complete each sentence.

1. If you want to make a telephone call, you need _____.

   a telephone number   **an operator**   **a pay phone**   **a calling card**

2. A country code is necessary for _____.

   a call from a pay phone   **a call from a cell phone**   **an international call**   **an operator-assisted call**

3. When you make a call to a business, they often put you _____.

   on the menu   **on hold**   **on a speakerphone**   **on call waiting**

4. If you need to send a document to someone, you can _____.

   call it in   **put it on hold**   **put in on voice mail**   **fax it**

| exercise | 18-4 |

Have you ever sent a fax? Explain how you did it.

First, _____

Then, _____

After that, _____

Finally, _____

| exercise | 18-5 |

Do you prefer to call your friends or to send them text messages? Why?

_____

_____

The Internet for Communicating

The **Internet** is another way to communicate with other people.

go/be online: *to use an Internet service to communicate with another person or people or to search or access sites on the Internet*

e-mail: *a system that allows you to send personal written messages to other people at their e-mail addresses from your e-mail address using a personal computer that is connected to the Internet; your e-mail address is assigned to you when you subscribe to an Internet service or sign up for e-mail through another company; computers where e-mail may be read or sent are made available to the public in such places as libraries, hotels, and Internet cafés. E-mail is so widely used that traditional mail through the post office is now called "snail mail" because it is so slow by comparison.*

user name/user ID: *a series of letters and/or numbers that you choose as your online identification; it is the first part of your e-mail address*

@: *(pronounced "at") the symbol that follows your user name in your e-mail address*

domain: *a common network name under which a collection of network devices are organized; the final part of your e-mail address is a period (pronounced "dot") plus the name of the domain; some examples are .com, .org, .edu (in the United States), and .mx (Mexico), .es (Spain), .uk (England)*

instant messaging/IM: *a service that allows you to send a message to someone who is online at the same time you are*

junk mail: *e-mail that you receive from someone unknown to you, often from an individual or business that would like to sell something to you*

spam: *junk mail that is designed to trick you or damage your computer*

virus: *a destructive computer program that copies and spreads itself via the Internet, causing damage to your computer*

malware: *software created with malicious intent that can harm the operation of a computer*

antivirus systems: *software that can be installed on your computer to block malware*

firewall: *a device used by an antivirus system that will help protect your computer from spam and malware*

video calling: *using special software, contacting someone who has the same software, enabling you both to see and talk to each other*

networking: *using the Internet to contact more than one person at a time*

social networks: *Internet groups that you can join and invite your friends and acquaintances to join so that you can keep in contact with each other in a semipublic way; there are also networks that enable (usually well-known) people to send instant messages to anyone in the general public who wishes to receive them*

blog: *a regular commentary made by an individual through a special Internet page*

online classes: *courses offered by many schools and universities that allow students to complete the required work by accessing the material, communicating with the teacher or professor, and taking exams through the Internet*

Many people send casual invitations by **e-mail**, but more formal ones by **snail mail**.

We were **online** at the same time and ended up **IM'ing** each other all afternoon.

My **antivirus software** requires continuous updates.

They have a **firewall** at work that rejects e-mails from unknown sources.

My neighbors are from Spain and use **video calling** to visit with their families every day.

When she was studying abroad, she wrote a **blog** describing all her adventures.

exercise 18-6

Complete each sentence with the most appropriate word or words.

1. In order to send an e-mail, you need _____.

   a firewall   **malware**   **a blog**   **an e-mail address**

2. You can get your own personal e-mail address from _____.

   a social network   **a videophone**   **an Internet service provider**   **a friend**

3. Domains based in the United States include _____.

   .es   **.edu**   **.mx**   **.aus**

4. When you are online, you can _____.

   make telephone calls   **send e-mails**   **print documents**   **all of the above**

Getting Information: The Media

Newspapers and Magazines

Newspapers and magazines are the traditional way to get local, national, and international news and information. Both can be bought at newsstands, supermarkets, and drugstores, and both are available for home delivery by subscription. Most newspapers and magazines are available online, and some offer material online that is not included in the printed issues.

Television for Getting Information

A television is a device that projects a still or moving image on its screen and delivers sound through its speakers. Television is a very popular way for people to get the news. There are also numerous programs on television that present commentary and analysis of the news from different points of view, in addition to talk shows where people discuss current issues. Cable or satellite television is a source for local government and civic programs that focus on events in local areas and make important public announcements in emergencies. Many educational and informative programs covering a wide range of topics are also available on television.

Types

high-definition television/HDTV/HD: *a television with high-resolution video, making the images on the screen clearer and showing more detail than older-style televisions*

flat screen/flat panel: *a slim television that can be hung on a wall or set on a pedestal*

plasma: *a flat screen television whose images are produced by gases contained in many tiny cells that are positioned between two plates of glass*

LCD: *television that uses liquid crystal display technology to produce images*

LED: *an LCD television that uses light-emitting diode backlighting instead of fluorescent lights*

Connections

plug-in: *a connection to an electrical outlet that enables you to receive a limited number of local programs with no fees*

cable: *a connection through an underground wiring system that enables you to receive hundreds of local, national, and international programs; this service is available in many areas and is provided by private companies, who charge a monthly fee*

dish: *a connection through a device that is placed on your roof or high on the side of your house and enables you to receive hundreds of programs; this service is available in many areas and is provided by private companies, who charge a monthly fee*

Internet-enabled TV: *a process by which you can download programs from the Internet directly to your television screen*

Using a Television

remote (control): *a handheld device that enables you to turn a television (or other appliance) on or off, change channels, adjust the volume, record programs, and control other connected apps from a distance*

arrow button: *a button on the remote that allows you to make changes to the television set-up or programming*

enter: *a button, usually located in the center of the arrow buttons on a remote, that you push to confirm your selection of a change*

DVR/digital video recorder: *an app for a television that enables you to record and save programs so that you can watch them later*

Plasma TVs are a little cheaper than **LEDs** and **LCDs**.

My friend doesn't have **cable** or a **dish**, but she can get lots of programs **downloaded** to her TV from the **Internet**.

We'll have to miss our favorite show, but we can save it on our **DVR** and watch it later.

The Internet for Getting Information

Almost any kind of information can be found on the Internet, which is made up of millions of **websites**.

website: *a page or pages of information about a business, government, other organization, or person made available on the Internet to anyone who wishes to read it; accessed via a website address, also known as a URL (uniform resource locator)*

Web page: *a page on a website*

HTML: *the standard that controls how Web pages are formatted and displayed*

hyperlink: *a reference to, and address of, another website where you can find more information about a topic mentioned on a website or Web page; clicking on the hyperlink or "link" will take you to this website*

search engine/browser: *a software application that is used to locate and display Web pages; a search engine may be found through its website address*

http://: *the first part of a website address, an abbreviation of "hypertext transfer protocol"; HTTP defines how messages are formatted and transmitted and what actions Web servers and browsers should take in response to various commands*

www.: *World Wide Web; the second part of a website address*

.com/.org/.edu/.org/.mx/.es/.uk/etc.: *names of domains; the final part of a website address; pronounced "dot com," "dot e-d-u," "dot org," "dot u-k," etc.*

user ID: *a name or e-mail address that identifies the person using the Internet*

password: *a second identification code, usually made up of letters and numbers, that is used to help ensure that the person using the Internet site is really the person to whom a user name belongs; you decide what your password is for each site you contact, and you should keep it a secret to protect your privacy and to help ensure that another person does not make any transaction in your name*

Verbs

scroll: *to move up or down a page on the computer screen using the mouse or touch pad*

surf: *to do research on or explore the Internet*

click: *to press one of the mouse or touch pad buttons and open a website*

enter: *to click on a button that will enable your information to be processed*

download: *to make a website visible on your computer screen*

upload: *to send your information to a website*

streaming: *getting continuous download from the Internet so that there is no program interruption*

It's convenient to get news on the **Internet**, but many people prefer to hold a real **newspaper** or **magazine** in their hands.

Their band is looking for someone to help them design a **Web page**.

Is it safe to **upload** your credit card number to a secure **website**?

exercise 19-1

Choose the most appropriate word or words to complete the following sentences.

1. Web page formats are controlled by _____.

   http   **www.**   **.com**   **HTML**

2. To do business through the Internet, you need a _____.

   hyperlink   **user ID**   **user ID**   **password**
                                             and password

3. "Surfing" is a way to _____.

   upload data   **get information** **read your e-mail** **get a user ID**

4. When you have decided on a password, you should _____.

   keep it a secret **post it on your** **tape it to**   **give it only to your**   **all of the**
                         Web page   **your computer**   **friends on a secure**   **previous**
                                                                   social networking site **answers**

Entertainment

Television/TV for Entertainment

Types of Video Entertainment Provided Electronically

movies: *films that are also shown in theaters and/or on television*

DVD/digital video disc: *a round, flat unit (disc) that stores large amounts of information—usually in the form of video—and can be played on a computer or with a DVD player connected to a television*

Blu-ray disc: *a round, flat unit, the same size as a CD or a DVD, that can be played with a Blu-ray player and has more than five times as much storage capacity as a DVD*

video games: *entertainment for one or more people, ranging from mental puzzles to highly physical activity*

computer games: *puzzle-type pastimes often based on traditional card games, games that require hand-eye coordination, games that allow the player to act out a role, and those that allow more than one player to participate*

game consoles: *apps that can be connected to a television that enable you to play a wide range of games, follow exercise programs, learn dance moves, download movies and music—actually to pursue almost any type of entertainment you can think of*

Audio Devices

Audio devices allow you to listen to music, the spoken word, or other sounds.

radio: *a device that transmits sounds by electric waves without wires; provides varied programs that offer music, news reports, commentary, comedy shows, theater, interviews, and so on through public broadcasts; radios are often built into cars and portable devices*

CD player: *a device, often built into a computer or a car, which plays CDs*

boom box: *a portable device that has a built-in radio and CD player and can be plugged in to an electrical outlet or powered by batteries*

MP3 player: *a small device that comes equipped with earphones and enables you to listen to music anywhere; you can plug an MP3 player into a computer and, for a fee, transfer music to it from the Internet; some MP3 players also provide electronic games*

Reading Devices/Electronic Books/E-Readers

Handheld reading devices are equipped with a screen on which the pages of a book can be displayed, enabling you to purchase, read, and store books electronically.

Cameras

digital camera: *a camera that enables you to capture images (like still photographs), without using film, that can be viewed, stored, and printed from your computer; many cell phones have a digital camera built in, but an individual camera usually produces higher-quality images*

digital camcorder: *a video camera that enables you to capture moving images (like motion pictures/movies), without using film, that can be viewed on a computer or projected onto a screen as well as stored in your computer*

exercise   20-1

Choose the most appropriate word or words to complete the following sentences.

1. If you want to walk down the street listening to music, you can carry _____.

   a boom box   **an MP3 player**   **a portable radio**   **all of the above**

2. You can select the type of entertainment you want on your television by using _____.

   a boom box   **a dish**   **a remote control**   **an MP3 player**

3. E-readers are useful while you are traveling because _____.

   you have access to a large number of books   **you can watch movies on them**   **they have built-in cameras**   **none of the above**

exercise   20-2

Make a list of the items listed in this section that you own or use regularly. After each one, write the brand name and tell what you use it for.

_____

_____

_____

Technology in Other Places

For Traveling

GPS/Global Positioning System: *a device that gives directions to a specified destination using on-screen instructions or a voice to tell the driver when and where to turn and give other important driving details; these devices are also useful on a boat, and walkers can use portable, handheld ones; some cell phones have a GPS built in*

Other apps: *different apps allow you to use the Internet, check e-mail, and stream television from a device installed in your car; most modern car engines are also built, tuned, and repaired with the use of computers*

e-tickets: *airline tickets that you purchase online and print out before you leave for the airport*

airport check-in: *a system that enables you to confirm your flight and print out your boarding pass using your computer and printer before you leave for the airport*

airport scanner: *a machine that inspects your baggage or your body for security purposes before you board an airplane*

For Banking

ATM/automatic teller machine: *a machine, located at a bank, shopping center, airport, or other convenient place, that enables you to deposit or withdraw money with the use of a special ATM card issued by your bank*

online banking: *using a connection to the Internet to do all of your business with your bank, including paying bills, moving money from one account to another, tracking loan payments, and so on*

For Shopping

credit card: *a plastic card with a number issued by a bank that allows you to purchase items without paying cash, then pay for them at the end of the month in one transaction; high interest charges are made if the bill is not paid in full by a certain date*

debit card: *a plastic card similar to a credit card issued by a bank that allows you to purchase items without paying cash; the amount you spend is immediately deducted from your bank account*

self checkout: *machines at checkout lines (usually in grocery stores) that enable you to pay quickly without the assistance of a cashier*

price check: *a machine placed in a store that allows you to electronically find the price of an item for sale there*

Internet shopping: *purchasing products through the Internet using a credit card*

Everywhere Else

Electronic devices affect practically every area of our lives. In our homes, **garage door openers, programmed heating, air-conditioning,** and other **appliances, security systems, baby monitors—** even our **children's toys—**are more and more based on ever-changing technology. The same is true regarding our health care, with machines that see inside our bodies, such as **MRI (magnetic resonance imaging)** and **CAT (computerized axial tomography) scan** machines and others that inspect our skin, bones, eyes, and teeth; **radiation** machines, **heart pumps, laser surgery,** and **electronic hearing aids** are just a few of the many ways that technology has helped improve the quality of our lives. Art and music have been transformed. Our schools are incorporating technology in an effort to improve learning. In our towns and cities, among many other functions, electronic devices control traffic and enable the police to fight crime. Offices cannot function without the use of electronic devices, and industry depends on technology in the manufacture of almost everything. In short, without technology, our lives would be brought to a standstill.

A good **GPS** can be a lifesaver when you are lost.

By using **ATMs** when you travel to another country, you can avoid having to change your cash into local currency.

Often if you don't find what you want in a store, you can find it and purchase it **online.**

exercise	21-1

1. Make a list of the items or services listed in Unit 21 that you own or use regularly. After each one, write the brand name and tell what you use it for. (Most people refer to their electronic devices by their brand names.)

_____

_____

_____

_____

2. Write a paragraph explaining how your life has changed in the past ten years because of new technology.

_____

_____

_____

_____

3. Challenge #1: Go through this entire section—Part V, Units 17 through 21—and identify all of the items that are sold under brand names. See if you can list the brands that are currently on the market.

_____

_____

_____

_____

4. Challenge #2: Make a list of any other new technological products and devices you find. Update your list as often as necessary.

_____

_____

_____

_____

Answer Key

Part I Nouns
Unit 1 People and Places

1-1
1. grandmother
2. grandfather
3. aunt
4. uncle
5. cousin
6. son-in-law
7. Answers will vary.
8. Answers will vary.

1-2
1. f
2. g
3. i.
4. d
5. h
6. e
7. a
8. c
9. b

1-3
1. doctor
2. police officer
3. neighbor
4. pharmacist
5. dentist

1-4
1. cheeks . . . chin . . . ears . . . eyes . . . face . . . hair . . . lips . . . mouth . . . nose
2. arm
3. knee
4. wrist
5. ankle
6. toes . . . fingers . . . thumb
7. neck . . . arm
8. waist

1-5
1. road
2. library
3. sun
4. farm
5. apartment
6. moon
7. post office
8. highway

1-6
Answers will vary.

1-7
Answers will vary.

1-8
Answers will vary.

1-9
Answers will vary.

1-10

1. bathroom
2. bedroom
3. bedroom
4. classroom
5. bedroom
6. any room
7. any room
8. dining room
9. classroom, office
10. any room
11. bathroom, bedroom, hall, kitchen
12. kitchen
13. living room
14. library, office
15. library, office
16. kitchen, restaurant, store
17. dining room, kitchen, restaurant, any room
18. classroom, office
19. kitchen, laundry room
20. dining room, kitchen, restaurant
21. kitchen, restaurant
22. bedroom
23. laundry room
24. department store
25. department store
26. bathroom
27. office
28. office
29. living room
30. dining room, kitchen, restaurant
31. kitchen, restaurant
32. dining room, kitchen, restaurant, any room
33. dining room, kitchen, restaurant

34. any room
35. any room
36. kitchen, restaurant
37. dining room, kitchen, restaurant
38. any room
39. bedroom
40. classroom, office, any room
41. kitchen, restaurant
42. classroom, office, any room
43. classroom, office, any room
44. classroom, office, any room
45. bedroom, living room
46. bedroom
47. kitchen, dining room, restaurant
48. classroom, library, office
49. kitchen, restaurant
50. kitchen, dining room, restaurant
51. bedroom
52. bathroom
53. bathroom, kitchen, laundry room, restaurant
54. bathroom, kitchen, laundry room
55. living room
56. dining room, kitchen, restaurant
57. hall
58. kitchen, restaurant
59. any room
60. kitchen
61. any room
62. kitchen, restaurant
63. bathroom
64. bathroom, kitchen
65. bedroom, living room, any room
66. laundry room

Unit 2 Singular, Plural, and Noncount Nouns

2-1

1. a
2. an
3. an
4. an
5. a
6. a
7. a
8. an
9. a
10. a

11. a
12. an
13. a
14. a
15. an
16. an
17. an
18. a
19. an
20. an

21. a
22. a
23. a
24. an
25. a
26. an
27. an
28. a
29. a
30. a

31. an
32. an
33. an
34. a
35. an
36. a
37. a
38. an
39. an
40. an

2-2

1. I have a book.
2. There is an answer key.
3. There is a *t*.
4. There is one *e*.

2-3

1. a class
2. a band . . . an orchestra
3. a company
4. a family

5. a team
6. a government
7. a committee
8. a choir . . . a chorus

2-4

1. brothers
2. daughters
3. wives
4. babies
5. children
6. men
7. women
8. teenagers
9. artists
10. customers
11. students
12. actresses
13. bosses
14. nurses
15. eyes
16. ears
17. toes
18. churches
19. cities
20. libraries
21. bus stops
22. post offices
23. windows
24. glasses
25. knives
26. forks
27. stoves
28. facecloths

2-5

1. bands
2. choirs
3. choruses
4. classes
5. committees
6. families
7. governments
8. orchestras
9. teams

2-6

Answers will vary.

2-7

Answers will vary.

2-8

Answers will vary.

2-9

1. an OR one . . . a OR one
2. an OR one . . . an OR one
3. some OR a lot of OR a few OR any . . . some OR a lot of OR a few OR any OR two
4. a OR one . . . some OR a few OR a lot of
5. a OR one
6. some OR two OR a few
7. any
8. some OR a lot of OR a few OR two
9. some OR a few OR two
10. a . . . some OR two

2-10

Answers will vary.

2-11

Answers will vary.

2-12

Answers will vary.

2-13

Answers will vary.

2-14

1. a little, a lot of, some, no, a slice of
2. three slices of
3. a little, some, three bowls of, a gallon of, two quarts of
4. a glass of, three glasses of, some, a little
5. some, a little, two bags of
6. a piece of, two pieces of, a little, some
7. some, a piece of, two pieces of, a lot of
8. some, a piece of, no
9. two, a few, some, no
10. a glass of, two glasses of, some, a lot of

2-15

Answers will vary.

2-16

1. a little
2. no, some, a little
3. some, a lot of
4. some, a little
5. too much, a lot of

2-17

Answers will vary.

2-18
1. an
2. Ø
3. Ø
4. Ø . . . Ø
5. Ø
6. a . . . Ø . . . a
7. Ø
8. Ø
9. Ø
10. a . . . a

2-19
1. a
2. the
3. Ø
4. the
5. Ø
6. the
7. the
8. the
9. Ø
10. the

2-20 Answers will vary.

2-21 Answers will vary.

2-22 Answers will vary.

2-23
1. a
2. Ø
3. The
4. Ø
5. the

2-24
1. This
2. those
3. that
4. these
5. that
6. those
7. these
8. this

Unit 3 Proper Nouns

3-1
1. She's reading a book called *A Guide to Good Manners.*
2. We have to go to the **S**pringfield **L**ibrary on **M**onday.
3. They are from **I**taly, and they don't speak **S**panish.
4. **D**avid is going to go to **W**ilson **A**cademy for **B**oys in **S**eptember.

3-2 Answers will vary.

Unit 4 Possessive Nouns and Pronouns

4-1
1. my sister's car
2. the men's hats
3. the children's party
4. the doctor's office
5. the girls' apartment
6. Miss Smith's class
7. Ben Lindsay's school
8. the ladies' meeting

4-2 Answers will vary.

4-3
1. her car
2. their hats
3. their party
4. his/her office
5. their apartment
6. her class
7. his school
8. their meeting

4-4 Answers will vary.

Unit 5 Review of Singular, Plural, and Noncount Nouns

5-1

1. too many	5. a little	9. John's
2. an	6. a lot of	10. some
3. the	7. too much	
4. Those	8. no	

5-2

1. one bottle/four bottles
2. these letters/that information
3. a few pills/a little medicine
4. too much sugar/one spoonful/a few spoonfuls
5. too many chairs/not much furniture/a chair
6. a necklace/these earrings/a little jewelry
7. that fruit/those vegetables
8. There is a nail/There are screws/There is hardware
9. There is one lamp/There are no lights/There is no water
10. Here is your letter/There are no letters

Unit 6 Verbs Used as Nouns

6-1

1. waiting	4. cooking
2. Driving	5. Studying
3. living	6. staying

6-2   Answers will vary.

Unit 7 More Specific Nouns

7-1

1. boys OR girls OR kids
2. dude OR guy OR youth
3. young lady
4. bum

7-2

1. fiancé
2. roommate
3. coworkers OR colleagues
4. acquaintance

7-3

1. e	6. c OR f OR g
2. c OR g	7. g
3. b OR c OR g	8. b OR c OR g
4. c OR g OR h	9. a
5. d	10. a OR i

7-4   Answers will vary.

7-5   Answers will vary.

7-6   Answers will vary.

7-7   Answers will vary.

7-8

1. d
2. f
3. e
4. b
5. a
6. c

7-9

Answers will vary.

7-10

1. g
2. b
3. h
4. f
5. d
6. j
7. e
8. a
9. c

7-11

1. e
2. f
3. b
4. h
5. a
6. d
7. g
8. c

7-12

Answers will vary.

7-13

Answers will vary.

7-14

Answers will vary.

7-15

Answers will vary.

7-16

Answers will vary.

7-17

1. c
2. d
3. a
4. e
5. f
6. b

7-18

1. hurricane
2. gale
3. sandstorm
4. tornado

Part II Adjectives
Unit 8 Making Descriptions

8-1

Answers will vary.

8-2

1. handicapped
2. shy
3. little
4. cowardly
5. ugly
6. slow
7. thin
8. unfriendly
9. stingy

8-3

1. bad
2. boring
3. small
4. energetic
5. kind
6. young
7. plain
8. humble
9. noisy

8-4

1. poor
2. serious
3. dumb
4. easygoing
5. bitter
6. short
7. happy
8. strong

8-5

1. incapable	9. impatient	17. undisciplined	25. unpleasant
2. incompetent	10. impolite	18. unenthusiastic	26. unpopular
3. inconsiderate	11. improper	19. unfaithful	27. unreasonable
4. inefficient	12. irresistible	20. unfortunate	28. unselfish
5. insecure	13. irreverent	21. unhappy	29. unsuccessful
6. insincere	14. unbalanced	22. unhealthy	30. untidy
7. intolerant	15. uncivil	23. unkind	31. untrustworthy
8. immodest	16. uncivilized	24. unnatural	32. untruthful

8-6

1. careless	4. unsuccessful
2. unfaithful	5. tactless
3. harmless	6. untruthful

8-7

1. intelligent	6. likable	11. optimistic	16. lovely	21. imaginative
2. persistent	7. responsible	12. pessimistic	17. lively	22. manipulative
3. independent	8. adorable	13. athletic	18. cowardly	23. persuasive
4. insistent	9. gullible	14. materialistic	19. friendly	24. aggressive
5. hospitable	10. flexible	15. idealistic	20. lonely	25. appreciative

8-8

1. a	4. a
2. an	5. an
3. an	

8-9

Answers will vary.

8-10

Answers will vary.

8-11

1. hungry	4. thirsty
2. busy	5. upset
3. ready	6. cold

8-12

1. anxious/upset/nervous	6. full
2. hot	7. dissatisfied
3. alive	8. well
4. clean	9. rested
5. sad/depressed	10. cool

8-13

Answers will vary.

8-14

1. narrow	4. tiny
2. big/large	5. short
3. light	

8-15

Answers will vary.

8-16

Answers will vary.

8-17

Answers will vary.

8-18

1. h	5. c	9. l
2. a	6. d	10. e
3. i	7. g	11. k
4. b	8. j	12. f

8-19
1. empty
2. new
3. patched
4. messy
5. dirty
6. broken
7. fresh

8-20 Answers will vary.

8-21
1. expensive
2. spacious
3. empty
4. dry
5. safe
6. light
7. unfurnished
8. well-maintained
9. open
10. old-fashioned

8-22 Answers will vary.

8-23
Pleasant: breezy, clear, cool, dry, nice, pleasant, sunny, warm
Unpleasant: chilly, cloudy, cold, foggy, freezing, hot, humid, icy, rainy, stormy, unpleasant, windy

8-24
1. freezing (Answers may vary.)
2. cold OR freezing OR icy OR unpleasant
3. pleasant (Answers may vary.)
4. Answers will vary.
5. hot (Answers may vary.)
6. foggy OR icy OR rainy OR stormy
7. rainy
8. cold OR freezing OR sunny
9. breezy OR windy
10. chilly

Unit 9 Comparisons and Superlatives

9-1
1. pretty
2. not at all
3. very
4. very
5. pretty

9-2 Answers will vary.

9-3 These are possible answers, but all may vary.
1. I didn't eat it.
2. We stayed home.
3. I got sick.
4. She got a ticket.
5. I'm not going to buy them.

9-4 Answers will vary.

9-5
1. brighter
2. cheaper
3. cleaner
4. colder
5. cooler
6. damper
7. darker
8. faster
9. fresher
10. higher
11. lighter
12. longer
13. neater
14. newer
15. older
16. plainer
17. poorer
18. richer
19. shorter
20. sicker
21. slower
22. smaller
23. smarter
24. sweeter
25. taller
26. younger

9-6
1. cuter
2. finer
3. lamer
4. looser
5. nicer
6. paler
7. ruder
8. tamer
9. wider

9-7
1. bigger
2. fatter
3. fitter
4. hotter
5. madder
6. redderv
7. sadder
8. thinner

9-8   Answers will vary.

9-9
1. angrier	7. dirtier	13. lonelier	19. sillier
2. bossier	8. easier	14. lovelier	20. sunnier
3. busier	9. friendlier	15. luckier	21. tastier
4. cloudier	10. funnier	16. noisier	22. uglier
5. cozier	11. happier	17. prettier	
6. crazier	12. lazier	18. rainier	

9-10
1. quieter	4. gentler
2. simpler	5. crueler
3. narrower	6. littler

9-11
1. more athletic	11. fresher	21. more proper	31. smaller
2. more boring	12. friendlier	22. prouder	32. stingier
3. more civil	13. gentler	23. quieter	33. more successful
4. more civilized	14. more gullible	24. ruder	34. sweeter
5. cleaner	15. healthier	25. sadder	35. tinier
6. more comfortable	16. hotter	26. more serious	36. more unfriendly
7. more considerate	17. more open	27. sicker	37. more upset
8. cooler	18. more patient	28. sillier	38. more useful
9. more delicious	19. more persuasive	29. more sincere	39. wider
10. dirtier	20. more pleasant	30. slower	40. more worried

9-12
1. prettier than	4. better than
2. not as comfortable as	5. not as big as
3. not as good as	

9-13
1. worst	5. cutest	9. hottest	13. neatest
2. cleanest	6. friendliest	10. silliest	14. nicest
3. coldest	7. gentlest	11. luckiest	15. rudest
4. craziest	8. best	12. maddest	16. saddest

9-14   Answers will vary.

9-15
1. most active	7. most generous	13. most serious
2. worst	8. happiest	14. ugliest
3. coldest	9. largest	15. most uninteresting
4. most comfortable	10. littlest	16. most useless
5. fastest	11. newest	
6. most flexible	12. noisiest	

9-16   Answers will vary.

Unit 10 Verbs and Nouns Used as Adjectives

10-1
1. boring	3. terrifying	5. confusing
2. frustrating	4. gratifying	6. daring

10-2
1. written	3. stolen	5. grown	7. Woven	9. forbidden
2. spoken	4. drunk	6. wounded	8. worn	10. withdrawn

10-3
1. fascinating
2. interested
3. surprising
4. confusing
5. terrified
6. excited
7. captivated
8. satisfied
9. frustrating
10. inspired

10-4
1. a necklace made of gold
2. a hook made of metal
3. a tray made of plastic
4. a bracelet made of silver
5. a floor made of oak
6. a basket made of wicker
7. a road made of dirt
8. a blouse made of silk
9. a skirt made of wool
10. a blanket made of cotton

10-5
1. a box for jewelry
2. a tray for ashes
3. a can for trash
4. a frame for a picture
5. a sack for flour
6. a ring for keys
7. a bag for groceries
8. a compartment for gloves
9. a box to carry your lunch in
10. a pail for garbage

10-6
1. for cracking nuts
2. for opening cans
3. for extinguishing (putting out) fires
4. for playing CDs
5. for breaking up ice
6. for drying hair
7. for removing nail polish
8. for sharpening pencils
9. for removing spots
10. for polishing floors

10-7
Answers will vary.

10-8
1. a bicycle lock
2. a mailbox key
3. a rose garden
4. homework
5. a student desk

10-9
1. hardheaded
2. sure-footed
3. single-minded
4. long-winded
5. evenhanded
6. hotheaded

10-10
1. a plan for the next five years
2. a warranty that lasts three years
3. a guarantee that lasts as long as you are living
4. a discussion that lasts ten minutes
5. a weight (or dumbbell) that weighs three pounds
6. a vacation that lasts two weeks
7. a contract for two years
8. a meeting that lasts all day
9. a party that lasts all night
10. something that happens every day

Unit 11 Adjective Order

11-1
1. a long black silk skirt
2. new Italian leather shoes
3. beautiful Mexican silver earrings
4. a rich three-layer birthday cake
5. a heavy round antique mirror

11-2
Answers will vary.

Part III Verbs
Unit 12 The Verb *Be*

12-1
1. is
2. are
3. is
4. are
5. are
6. am

12-2
Answers will vary.

12-3
1. Is he here now?
2. Are you happy?
3. Am I sitting down?
4. Is he asking directions?
5. Are they building a new house?
6. Is she turning left?
7. Is he taking photographs?
8. Is she riding a bicycle?

12-4
1. He isn't here now.
2. You're not happy.
3. I'm not sitting down.
4. He isn't asking directions.
5. They aren't building a new house.
6. She isn't turning left.
7. He isn't taking photographs.
8. She isn't riding a bicycle.

12-5
1. was
2. were
3. was
4. were
5. were
6. was

12-6
Answers will vary but should include these verbs.
1. I was . . .
2. . . . was with me.
3. I was . . . OR We were . . .
4. It was . . .
5. No, nobody else was there. OR Yes, _____ was there. OR Yes, _____ and _____ were there.

Unit 13 Non–*To Be* Verbs

13-1
1. h
2. i
3. e
4. j
5. f
6. g
7. a
8. b
9. d
10. c

13-2
1. sounds
2. appear
3. feel
4. smell
5. seems
6. resembles

13-3
1. matches
2. eats
3. has
4. drinks
5. goes
6. wishes
7. cleans
8. dries
9. does
10. dances

13-4
1. cleaned
2. opened
3. worked
4. walked
5. watched

13-5
1. stopped
2. closed
3. shopped
4. exercised
5. tried

13-6
1. listened
2. laughed
3. turned
4. dreamed
5. cried
6. exercised
7. brushed
8. smiled
9. planned
10. watched

13-7
Answers will vary.

13-8
Answers will vary.

13-9
Answers will vary.

13-10
1. makes
2. water
3. clean
4. vacuum
5. pays

13-11
Answers will vary.

13-12
Answers will vary.

13-13
1. sweep the floor
2. do the shopping
3. iron clothes
4. make appointments
5. wash the windows OR clean up the mess
6. pay bills
7. make repairs
8. clean up the yard OR mow the lawn OR take out the trash OR water plants OR weed the garden
9. do laundry
10. dust the furniture

13-14
Answers will vary.

13-15
1. answered
2. asked
3. corrected
4. erased
5. helped
6. learned
7. listened
8. paid
9. played
10. solved
11. spelled
12. studied
13. used

13-16
1. taught
2. wrote
3. understood
4. took
5. made
6. did
7. drew
8. took
9. read
10. paid

13-17
1. He doesn't get up at 6:00.
2. They don't eat breakfast together every morning.
3. She doesn't dream during the day.
4. We don't buy groceries every week.
5. I don't laugh a lot.

13-18
1. My mother didn't teach me to read and write.
2. He didn't write her an e-mail last week.
3. I didn't understand today's lesson.
4. We didn't take a hard test this morning.
5. You didn't make only one mistake.
6. They didn't do all of the exercises.
7. They didn't draw pictures in class.
8. My friend and I didn't take turns with the computer.
9. She didn't read us a wonderful story.
10. I hope you didn't pay attention.

13-19   Answers will vary.

13-20   Answers will vary.

13-21
1. Do you write e-mail?
2. Does he search the Internet?
3. Does she use the computer?
4. Do you all attend meetings?
5. Do they answer the telephone?
6. Do we take coffee breaks?

13-22
1. What goes in that file?
2. Who answers the telephone?
3. When do you search the Internet?
4. Where do we send faxes?
5. Where do they write the reports?

13-23
1. Did they take a long coffee break?
2. Did she answer the telephone?
3. Did Mary write these e-mails?
4. Did you search the Internet this afternoon?
5. Did John organize all your files?

13-24
1. Who wrote a letter today?
2. What did he do yesterday?
3. When did John call you?
4. Where did you eat on Monday night?
5. How did she go home?

13-25   Answers will vary.

13-26   Answers will vary.

13-27   Answers will vary.

13-28   Answers will vary.

13-29
1. Do you return clothes that don't fit?
2. Does she always use her credit card?
3. Does she like her new shoes?
4. Do you want these shirts?
5. Does he like to go shopping?

13-30
1. Did she buy a new dress?
2. Did he forget to give you a receipt?
3. Did you try on a lot of clothes?
4. Did she go shopping yesterday?
5. Did you buy anything?

13-31
1. Who always gets a bargain?
2. What did you do for thirty minutes?
3. Where did they spend a lot of money?
4. Who does he always thank?
5. When did you write the check?
6. How much did it cost?

13-32
1. lost my checkbook
2. drove up to the drive-up window
3. make a deposit
4. withdraw cash
5. buy a CD

13-33
1. They didn't close their account.
2. This account doesn't earn interest.
3. I didn't get a new PIN.
4. He didn't withdraw cash.
5. She doesn't make a deposit every week.

13-34
1. Did you pay an installment last month?
2. Did you want to open an account?
3. When did she buy a CD?
4. What did he do?
5. Who withdrew cash?

13-35 Answers will vary.

13-36
1. He is cashing a check.
2. I am withdrawing money.
3. They are opening an account.
4. We are applying for a loan.
5. The investment is earning interest.
6. She is getting cash from the ATM.
7. I am saving money.
8. He is paying an installment on his loan.

13-37 Answers will vary.

13-38 Answers will vary.

13-39
1. Where did you have a picnic?
2. Who gets off the bus here?
3. Did he take a lot of photographs?
4. Did she lie in the sun for an hour?
5. What does he always buy?

13-40
1. She doesn't ask directions.
2. We don't turn left here.
3. He doesn't drive a car.
4. They don't get lost.
5. I don't go jogging.

13-41
1. We didn't see an accident.
2. They didn't have a picnic.
3. He didn't get on the bus.
4. You didn't turn right.
5. She didn't get out of the car.

13-42
1. was, were
2. became
3. built
4. bought
5. came
6. did
7. drew
8. drank
9. drove
10. ate
11. felt
12. found
13. got
14. went
15. grew
16. had
17. heard
18. lay
19. made
20. paid
21. put
22. left
23. read
24. rode
25. ran
26. saw
27. sat
28. slept
29. spent
30. stood
31. swept
32. took
33. taught
34. thought
35. understood
36. woke up
37. withdrew
38. wrote

13-43
1. He is getting off the elevator.
2. We are ordering our meal.
3. She is paying the waiter.
4. We are leaving the station.
5. They are going through the revolving doors.

13-44
1. He isn't leaving the building.
2. She isn't enjoying her meal.
3. They aren't riding on the escalator.
4. I'm not looking at the menu.
5. He's not talking on his cell phone.

13-45
1. Is he leaving the building?
2. Is she enjoying her meal?
3. Are they riding on the escalator?
4. Are you looking at the menu?
5. Is he talking on his cell phone?

13-46
1. She hasn't asked directions.
2. We haven't turned left here.
3. He hasn't driven a car.
4. They haven't gotten lost.
5. I haven't gone jogging.

13-47
1. ate
2. eaten
3. understand
4. understood
5. write
6. written
7. took
8. taken
9. be
10. was, were
11. teach
12. taught
13. came
14. come

13-48
1. I haven't eaten dinner.
2. She hasn't left the station.
3. We haven't looked at the menu.
4. He hasn't ordered his lunch.

5. She has paid the waiter.
6. We haven't bought anything from a street vendor.
7. I have asked for the check.

13-49
1. The game is beginning.
2. He is swimming.
3. They are winning.

4. She is throwing the ball.
5. We are singing together.
6. I am going to the movies.

13-50
1. Is the game beginning?
2. Is he swimming?
3. Are they winning?

4. Is she throwing the ball?
5. Are you singing together?
6. Are you going to the movies?

13-51
1. He hasn't hit the ball.
2. I haven't seen that movie.
3. She hasn't had lunch with him.

4. We haven't sung that song.
5. They haven't danced together before.

13-52
1. Has he hit the ball?
2. Have you seen that movie?
3. Has she had lunch with him?

4. Have you/we sung that song?
5. Have they danced together before?

13-53
Answers will vary.

13-54
Answers will vary.

13-55
1. 3	5. 2	9. 1
2. 2	6. 3	10. 1
3. 1	7. 3	11. 2
4. 3	8. 1	12. 2

13-56
1. I added tomatoes to the sauce.
2. She iced and decorated the cakes in the morning.
3. He whipped the cream.

4. They cooked for a lot of people.
5. We grilled the fish outside.

13-57
1. Did you add tomatoes to the sauce?
2. Did she ice and decorate the cakes in the morning?
3. Did he whip the cream?

4. Did they cook for a lot of people?
5. Did you grill the fish outside?

13-58
1. We have barbecued the chicken.
2. She has removed the pan from the oven.
3. He has arranged the salad on the plates.

4. I have peeled the potatoes.
5. They have spread butter on the bread.

13-59
1. Slice
2. Ice
3. Remove
4. Spread
5. Chill
6. Break
7. Bake
8. Boil

13-60
1. I am slicing the tomatoes.
2. I am icing the cake.
3. I am removing the pan from the oven.
4. I am spreading butter on the bread.

5. I am chilling the champagne.
6. I am breaking the eggs into the bowl.
7. I am baking a loaf of bread.
8. I am boiling water for the tea.

Part IV Adverbs
Unit 14 Adverbs of Place, Time, and Frequency

14-1
1. g
2. a
3. e
4. b
5. c
6. d
7. h
8. f

14-2   Answers will vary.

14-3
1. there
2. here
3. there
4. inside
5. nearby
6. up
7. downstairs
8. outside

14-4
1. in the country
2. on a horse
3. in a car
4. on the fourth floor
5. in the kitchen
6. in jail
7. in the hospital
8. on a balcony OR on a deck OR on a patio
9. at school OR at the library
10. on a bicycle OR on a bus OR on a train OR on the metro

14-5   Answers will vary.

14-6
1. Yesterday
2. Tomorrow
3. next month
4. last month
5. this Friday
6. next year
7. ten years ago
8. this morning
9. this evening OR tonight
10. Answers will vary.

14-7
1. at 3:30
2. on weekdays
3. in March
4. in 2010
5. in the morning

14-8
1. i
2. d
3. h
4. g
5. c
6. e
7. j
8. k
9. f
10. b
11. a

14-9   Answers will vary.

14-10   Answers will vary.

Unit 15 Adverbs of Manner

15-1
1. actively
2. aggressively
3. badly
4. bitterly
5. bravely
6. carefully
7. cautiously
8. charmingly
9. cheaply
10. cheerfully
11. civilly
12. competently
13. considerately
14. creatively
15. efficiently
16. faithfully
17. fortunately
18. generously
19. gladly
20. imaginatively
21. interestingly
22. kindly
23. loudly
24. modestly
25. naturally
26. nervously
27. nicely
28. patiently
29. pleasantly
30. politely
31. properly
32. proudly
33. quietly
34. reverently
35. securely
36. selfishly
37. seriously
38. sincerely
39. skillfully
40. slowly
41. softly
42. successfully
43. sweetly
44. tactfully
45. truthfully
46. weakly

15-2

1. capably
2. comfortably
3. easily
4. energetically
5. enthusiastically
6. fast
7. well
8. humbly
9. happily
10. noisily
11. reasonably
12. responsibly
13. tragically

15-3

1. bravely
2. responsibly
3. easily
4. Fortunately
5. cheerfully
6. carefully
7. gladly
8. badly
9. creatively
10. patiently

15-4

Answers will vary.

15-5

1. John drives more slowly than Mary.
2. Susan works more carefully than Janet.
3. Charles plays more quietly than David.

15-6

Answers will vary.

15-7

1. Mary doesn't drive as slowly as John.
2. Janet doesn't work as carefully as Susan.
3. David doesn't play as quietly as Charles.

15-8

1. not as slowly as
2. faster than
3. not as quietly as
4. better than
5. not as energetically as
6. earlier than
7. not as efficiently as
8. more patiently than
9. not as hard as
10. more seriously than
11. not as late as
12. more sweetly than

15-9

Answers will vary.

15-10

Answers will vary.

Unit 16 Adverbs That Modify

16-1

1. really
2. hardly OR scarcely
3. really
4. hardly OR scarcely

16-2

1. well enough
2. well
3. a little OR well enough
4. a little OR well enough
5. well

16-3

Answers will vary.

16-4

1. pretty OR rather OR quite OR very
2. too OR extremely OR very
3. extremely OR very
4. pretty OR rather OR quite
5. not at all

16-5

Answers will vary.

16-6
1. Sara is much shorter than her brother.
2. Jackie is much friendlier than Susan.
3. Joe is much more helpful than Jim.
4. Mary is much more athletic than her sister.
5. Patricia's baby was much smaller than Valerie's.

16-7
Answers will vary.

16-8
Answers will vary.

Part V English in the Twenty-First Century: Technology
Unit 17 General Vocabulary for Technology

17-1
1. USB flash drive
2. toner
3. laptop
4. hard drive
5. keyboard

17-2
Answers will vary.

17-3
1. the Web
2. a modem
3. worldwide
4. Wi-Fi

17-4
1. an analog
2. touch screen
3. save
4. downloading

Unit 18 Contacting Other People: The Technology of Communications

18-1
1. an earphone
2. a ringer
3. printing a document
4. cell phone

18-2
Answers will vary.

18-3
1. a telephone number
2. an international call
3. on hold
4. fax it

18-4
Answers will vary.

18-5
Answers will vary.

18-6
1. an e-mail address
2. an Internet service provider
3. .edu
4. all of the above

Unit 19 Getting Information: The Media

19-1
1. HTML
2. user ID and password
3. get information
4. keep it a secret

Unit 20 Entertainment

20-1

1. all of the above
2. a remote control
3. you have access to a large number of books

20-2   Answers will vary.

Unit 21 Technology in Other Places

21-1   Answers will vary.